C-2997 **CAREER EXAMINATION SERIES**

T0379186

THIS IS YOUR **PASSBOOK**® FOR ...

TAX COMPLIANCE REPRESENTATIVE

NLC®

NATIONAL LEARNING CORPORATION®
passbooks.com

NLC®

National Learning Corporation

212 Michael Drive, Syosset, NY 11791
(516) 921-8888 • www.passbooks.com
E-mail: info@passbooks.com

PUBLISHED IN THE UNITED STATES OF AMERICA

PASSBOOK® SERIES

THE *PASSBOOK® SERIES* has been created to prepare applicants and candidates for the ultimate academic battlefield – the examination room.

At some time in our lives, each and every one of us may be required to take an examination – for validation, matriculation, admission, qualification, registration, certification, or licensure.

Based on the assumption that every applicant or candidate has met the basic formal educational standards, has taken the required number of courses, and read the necessary texts, the *PASSBOOK® SERIES* furnishes the one special preparation which may assure passing with confidence, instead of failing with insecurity. Examination questions – together with answers – are furnished as the basic vehicle for study so that the mysteries of the examination and its compounding difficulties may be eliminated or diminished by a sure method.

This book is meant to help you pass your examination provided that you qualify and are serious in your objective.

The entire field is reviewed through the huge store of content information which is succinctly presented through a provocative and challenging approach – the question-and-answer method.

A climate of success is established by furnishing the correct answers at the end of each test.

You soon learn to recognize types of questions, forms of questions, and patterns of questioning. You may even begin to anticipate expected outcomes.

You perceive that many questions are repeated or adapted so that you can gain acute insights, which may enable you to score many sure points.

You learn how to confront new questions, or types of questions, and to attack them confidently and work out the correct answers.

You note objectives and emphases, and recognize pitfalls and dangers, so that you may make positive educational adjustments.

Moreover, you are kept fully informed in relation to new concepts, methods, practices, and directions in the field.

You discover that you arre actually taking the examination all the time: you are preparing for the examination by "taking" an examination, not by reading extraneous and/or supererogatory textbooks.

In short, this PASSBOOK®, used directedly, should be an important factor in helping you to pass your test.

TAX COMPLIANCE REPRESENTATIVE

DUTIES:

As a Tax Compliance Representative, under the supervision of a Tax Compliance Representative II, you would initially be assigned to one of the Department's collection desk operations working in an environment using the latest technology, software, and automated telephone operations to handle large volumes of incoming and outgoing phone calls and case inventory. You would interact with customers via inbound and outbound calls, and would be responsible for the collection of delinquent assessments and returns. This may require you to explain the collection process; access computer systems in order to provide detailed explanations of assessment(s), account adjustments, payments, and refunds; update taxpayer account information; answer questions concerning the provisions and requirements of the Tax Law; compute taxes, penalties, and interest due the State; prepare written responses to requests for information; follow up on taxpayers' cases; research Tax Laws and Regulations in commonly used reference materials; provide technical information on other collection options such as settlements; explain enforcement actions available to collect the debt; make address inquiries; and obtain information required to resolve cases. Other duties include but are not limited to negotiating payment arrangements, reviewing financial documentation, locating property and other assets of debtor, and initiating and determining the next step in collection actions including the service of levies. You would be expected to act in a calm, courteous, and reasonable manner even under very difficult, highly stressful, and at times, confrontational circumstances. 'All calls are subject to monitoring for quality assurance. You may be required to work a non-traditional work week, including evenings and/or weekends.

As a Tax Compliance Representative, Department of Labor, you would perform a variety of central office functions to effect the collection of delinquent Unemployment Insurance contributions, penalties, and interest, and obtain delinquent contribution returns from employers. Your duties would include, but would not be limited to, contacting employers; explaining provisions of the Unemployment Insurance Law; conducting office or telephone interviews with employers to collect overdue contribution returns and Unemployment Insurance contributions, penalties, and interest; maintaining a comprehensive case history of all assigned cases; and making recommendations for further action. You would also enforce the collection of delinquent Unemployment Insurance contributions, penalties, and interest through the filing of warrants, serving levies, income executions, and other appropriate collection mechanisms. In the performance of these assigned duties, you may interact with uncooperative or sometimes hostile individuals. You may also be required to work a non-traditional work week which may include evenings and/or weekends.

SUBJECT OF EXAMINATION:
The written test is designed to test for knowledge, skills, and/or abilities in such areas as:

1. **Evaluating conclusions in light of known facts** - These questions will consist of a set of factual statements and a conclusion. You must decide if the conclusion is proved by the facts, disproved by the facts or if the facts are not sufficient to prove or disprove the conclusion. The questions will not be specific to a particular field.
2. **Preparing written material** - These questions test for the ability to present information clearly and accurately, and to organize paragraphs logically and comprehensibly. For some questions, you will be given information in two or three sentences followed by four restatements of the information. You must then choose the best version. For other questions, you will be given paragraphs with their sentences out of order. You must then choose, from four suggestions, the best order for the sentences.
3. **Public contact principles and practices** - These questions test for knowledge of techniques used to interact with other people, to gather and present information, and to provide assistance, advice, and effective customer service in a courteous and professional manner. Questions will cover such topics as understanding and responding to people with diverse needs, perspectives, personalities, and levels of familiarity with agency operations, as well as acting in a way that both serves the public and reflects well on your agency.
4. **Understanding and interpreting tabular material** - These questions test your ability to understand, analyze, and use the internal logic of data presented in tabular form. You may be asked to perform tasks such as completing tables, drawing conclusions from them, analyzing data trends or interrelationships, and revising or combining data sets. The concepts of rate, ratio, and proportion are tested. Mathematical operations are simple, and computational speed is not a major factor in the test. You should bring with you a hand-held battery- or solar-powered calculator for use on this test. You will not be permitted to use the calculator function of your cell phone.
5. **Understanding and interpreting written material** - These questions test for the ability to understand and interpret information in the paragraph, and not what you may happen to know about the topic.

HOW TO TAKE A TEST

I. YOU MUST PASS AN EXAMINATION

A. WHAT EVERY CANDIDATE SHOULD KNOW

Examination applicants often ask us for help in preparing for the written test. What can I study in advance? What kinds of questions will be asked? How will the test be given? How will the papers be graded?

As an applicant for a civil service examination, you may be wondering about some of these things. Our purpose here is to suggest effective methods of advance study and to describe civil service examinations.

Your chances for success on this examination can be increased if you know how to prepare. Those "pre-examination jitters" can be reduced if you know what to expect. You can even experience an adventure in good citizenship if you know why civil service exams are given.

B. WHY ARE CIVIL SERVICE EXAMINATIONS GIVEN?

Civil service examinations are important to you in two ways. As a citizen, you want public jobs filled by employees who know how to do their work. As a job seeker, you want a fair chance to compete for that job on an equal footing with other candidates. The best-known means of accomplishing this two-fold goal is the competitive examination.

Exams are widely publicized throughout the nation. They may be administered for jobs in federal, state, city, municipal, town or village governments or agencies.

Any citizen may apply, with some limitations, such as the age or residence of applicants. Your experience and education may be reviewed to see whether you meet the requirements for the particular examination. When these requirements exist, they are reasonable and applied consistently to all applicants. Thus, a competitive examination may cause you some uneasiness now, but it is your privilege and safeguard.

C. HOW ARE CIVIL SERVICE EXAMS DEVELOPED?

Examinations are carefully written by trained technicians who are specialists in the field known as "psychological measurement," in consultation with recognized authorities in the field of work that the test will cover. These experts recommend the subject matter areas or skills to be tested; only those knowledges or skills important to your success on the job are included. The most reliable books and source materials available are used as references. Together, the experts and technicians judge the difficulty level of the questions.

Test technicians know how to phrase questions so that the problem is clearly stated. Their ethics do not permit "trick" or "catch" questions. Questions may have been tried out on sample groups, or subjected to statistical analysis, to determine their usefulness.

Written tests are often used in combination with performance tests, ratings of training and experience, and oral interviews. All of these measures combine to form the best-known means of finding the right person for the right job.

II. HOW TO PASS THE WRITTEN TEST

A. NATURE OF THE EXAMINATION

To prepare intelligently for civil service examinations, you should know how they differ from school examinations you have taken. In school you were assigned certain definite pages to read or subjects to cover. The examination questions were quite detailed and usually emphasized memory. Civil service exams, on the other hand, try to discover your present ability to perform the duties of a position, plus your potentiality to learn these duties. In other words, a civil service exam attempts to predict how successful you will be. Questions cover such a broad area that they cannot be as minute and detailed as school exam questions.

In the public service similar kinds of work, or positions, are grouped together in one "class." This process is known as *position-classification*. All the positions in a class are paid according to the salary range for that class. One class title covers all of these positions, and they are all tested by the same examination.

B. FOUR BASIC STEPS

1) Study the announcement

How, then, can you know what subjects to study? Our best answer is: "Learn as much as possible about the class of positions for which you've applied." The exam will test the knowledge, skills and abilities needed to do the work.

Your most valuable source of information about the position you want is the official exam announcement. This announcement lists the training and experience qualifications. Check these standards and apply only if you come reasonably close to meeting them.

The brief description of the position in the examination announcement offers some clues to the subjects which will be tested. Think about the job itself. Review the duties in your mind. Can you perform them, or are there some in which you are rusty? Fill in the blank spots in your preparation.

Many jurisdictions preview the written test in the exam announcement by including a section called "Knowledge and Abilities Required," "Scope of the Examination," or some similar heading. Here you will find out specifically what fields will be tested.

2) Review your own background

Once you learn in general what the position is all about, and what you need to know to do the work, ask yourself which subjects you already know fairly well and which need improvement. You may wonder whether to concentrate on improving your strong areas or on building some background in your fields of weakness. When the announcement has specified "some knowledge" or "considerable knowledge," or has used adjectives like "beginning principles of..." or "advanced ... methods," you can get a clue as to the number and difficulty of questions to be asked in any given field. More questions, and hence broader coverage, would be included for those subjects which are more important in the work. Now weigh your strengths and weaknesses against the job requirements and prepare accordingly.

3) Determine the level of the position

Another way to tell how intensively you should prepare is to understand the level of the job for which you are applying. Is it the entering level? In other words, is this the position in which beginners in a field of work are hired? Or is it an intermediate or advanced level? Sometimes this is indicated by such words as "Junior" or "Senior" in the class title. Other jurisdictions use Roman numerals to designate the level – Clerk I, Clerk II, for example. The word "Supervisor" sometimes appears in the title. If the level is not indicated by the title, check the description of duties. Will you be working under very close supervision, or will you have responsibility for independent decisions in this work?

4) Choose appropriate study materials

Now that you know the subjects to be examined and the relative amount of each subject to be covered, you can choose suitable study materials. For beginning level jobs, or even advanced ones, if you have a pronounced weakness in some aspect of your training, read a modern, standard textbook in that field. Be sure it is up to date and has general coverage. Such books are normally available at your library, and the librarian will be glad to help you locate one. For entry-level positions, questions of appropriate difficulty are chosen – neither highly advanced questions, nor those too simple. Such questions require careful thought but not advanced training.

If the position for which you are applying is technical or advanced, you will read more advanced, specialized material. If you are already familiar with the basic principles of your field, elementary textbooks would waste your time. Concentrate on advanced textbooks and technical periodicals. Think through the concepts and review difficult problems in your field.

These are all general sources. You can get more ideas on your own initiative, following these leads. For example, training manuals and publications of the government agency which employs workers in your field can be useful, particularly for technical and professional positions. A letter or visit to the government department involved may result in more specific study suggestions, and certainly will provide you with a more definite idea of the exact nature of the position you are seeking.

III. KINDS OF TESTS

Tests are used for purposes other than measuring knowledge and ability to perform specified duties. For some positions, it is equally important to test ability to make adjustments to new situations or to profit from training. In others, basic mental abilities not dependent on information are essential. Questions which test these things may not appear as pertinent to the duties of the position as those which test for knowledge and information. Yet they are often highly important parts of a fair examination. For very general questions, it is almost impossible to help you direct your study efforts. What we can do is to point out some of the more common of these general abilities needed in public service positions and describe some typical questions.

1) General information

Broad, general information has been found useful for predicting job success in some kinds of work. This is tested in a variety of ways, from vocabulary lists to questions about current events. Basic background in some field of work, such as sociology or economics, may be sampled in a group of questions. Often these are principles which have become familiar to most persons through exposure rather than through formal training. It is difficult to advise you how to study for these questions; being alert to the world around you is our best suggestion.

2) Verbal ability

An example of an ability needed in many positions is verbal or language ability. Verbal ability is, in brief, the ability to use and understand words. Vocabulary and grammar tests are typical measures of this ability. Reading comprehension or paragraph interpretation questions are common in many kinds of civil service tests. You are given a paragraph of written material and asked to find its central meaning.

3) Numerical ability

Number skills can be tested by the familiar arithmetic problem, by checking paired lists of numbers to see which are alike and which are different, or by interpreting charts and graphs. In the latter test, a graph may be printed in the test booklet which you are asked to use as the basis for answering questions.

4) Observation

A popular test for law-enforcement positions is the observation test. A picture is shown to you for several minutes, then taken away. Questions about the picture test your ability to observe both details and larger elements.

5) Following directions

In many positions in the public service, the employee must be able to carry out written instructions dependably and accurately. You may be given a chart with several columns, each column listing a variety of information. The questions require you to carry out directions involving the information given in the chart.

6) Skills and aptitudes

Performance tests effectively measure some manual skills and aptitudes. When the skill is one in which you are trained, such as typing or shorthand, you can practice. These tests are often very much like those given in business school or high school courses. For many of the other skills and aptitudes, however, no short-time preparation can be made. Skills and abilities natural to you or that you have developed throughout your lifetime are being tested.

Many of the general questions just described provide all the data needed to answer the questions and ask you to use your reasoning ability to find the answers. Your best preparation for these tests, as well as for tests of facts and ideas, is to be at your physical and mental best. You, no doubt, have your own methods of getting into an exam-taking mood and keeping “in shape.” The next section lists some ideas on this subject.

IV. KINDS OF QUESTIONS

Only rarely is the “essay” question, which you answer in narrative form, used in civil service tests. Civil service tests are usually of the short-answer type. Full instructions for answering these questions will be given to you at the examination. But in case this is your first experience with short-answer questions and separate answer sheets, here is what you need to know:

1) Multiple-choice Questions

Most popular of the short-answer questions is the "multiple choice" or "best answer" question. It can be used, for example, to test for factual knowledge, ability to solve problems or judgment in meeting situations found at work.

A multiple-choice question is normally one of three types—

- It can begin with an incomplete statement followed by several possible endings. You are to find the one ending which *best* completes the statement, although some of the others may not be entirely wrong.
- It can also be a complete statement in the form of a question which is answered by choosing one of the statements listed.
- It can be in the form of a problem – again you select the best answer.

Here is an example of a multiple-choice question with a discussion which should give you some clues as to the method for choosing the right answer:

When an employee has a complaint about his assignment, the action which will *best* help him overcome his difficulty is to

A. discuss his difficulty with his coworkers
B. take the problem to the head of the organization
C. take the problem to the person who gave him the assignment
D. say nothing to anyone about his complaint

In answering this question, you should study each of the choices to find which is best. Consider choice "A" – Certainly an employee may discuss his complaint with fellow employees, but no change or improvement can result, and the complaint remains unresolved. Choice "B" is a poor choice since the head of the organization probably does not know what assignment you have been given, and taking your problem to him is known as "going over the head" of the supervisor. The supervisor, or person who made the assignment, is the person who can clarify it or correct any injustice. Choice "C" is, therefore, correct. To say nothing, as in choice "D," is unwise. Supervisors have and interest in knowing the problems employees are facing, and the employee is seeking a solution to his problem.

2) True/False Questions

The "true/false" or "right/wrong" form of question is sometimes used. Here a complete statement is given. Your job is to decide whether the statement is right or wrong.

SAMPLE: A roaming cell-phone call to a nearby city costs less than a non-roaming call to a distant city.

This statement is wrong, or false, since roaming calls are more expensive.

This is not a complete list of all possible question forms, although most of the others are variations of these common types. You will always get complete directions for answering questions. Be sure you understand *how* to mark your answers – ask questions until you do.

V. RECORDING YOUR ANSWERS

Computer terminals are used more and more today for many different kinds of exams.

For an examination with very few applicants, you may be told to record your answers in the test booklet itself. Separate answer sheets are much more common. If this separate answer sheet is to be scored by machine – and this is often the case – it is highly important that you mark your answers correctly in order to get credit.

An electronic scoring machine is often used in civil service offices because of the speed with which papers can be scored. Machine-scored answer sheets must be marked with a pencil, which will be given to you. This pencil has a high graphite content which responds to the electronic scoring machine. As a matter of fact, stray dots may register as answers, so do not let your pencil rest on the answer sheet while you are pondering the correct answer. Also, if your pencil lead breaks or is otherwise defective, ask for another.

Since the answer sheet will be dropped in a slot in the scoring machine, be careful not to bend the corners or get the paper crumpled.

The answer sheet normally has five vertical columns of numbers, with 30 numbers to a column. These numbers correspond to the question numbers in your test booklet. After each number, going across the page are four or five pairs of dotted lines. These short dotted lines have small letters or numbers above them. The first two pairs may also have a "T" or "F" above the letters. This indicates that the first two pairs only are to be used if the questions are of the true-false type. If the questions are multiple choice, disregard the "T" and "F" and pay attention only to the small letters or numbers.

Answer your questions in the manner of the sample that follows:

32. The largest city in the United States is
    - A. Washington, D.C.
    - B. New York City
    - C. Chicago
    - D. Detroit
    - E. San Francisco

1) Choose the answer you think is best. (New York City is the largest, so "B" is correct.)
2) Find the row of dotted lines numbered the same as the question you are answering. (Find row number 32)
3) Find the pair of dotted lines corresponding to the answer. (Find the pair of lines under the mark "B.")
4) Make a solid black mark between the dotted lines.

VI. BEFORE THE TEST

Common sense will help you find procedures to follow to get ready for an examination. Too many of us, however, overlook these sensible measures. Indeed, nervousness and fatigue have been found to be the most serious reasons why applicants fail to do their best on civil service tests. Here is a list of reminders:

- Begin your preparation early – Don't wait until the last minute to go scurrying around for books and materials or to find out what the position is all about.
- Prepare continuously – An hour a night for a week is better than an all-night cram session. This has been definitely established. What is more, a night a week for a month will return better dividends than crowding your study into a shorter period of time.
- Locate the place of the exam – You have been sent a notice telling you when and where to report for the examination. If the location is in a different town or otherwise unfamiliar to you, it would be well to inquire the best route and learn something about the building.
- Relax the night before the test – Allow your mind to rest. Do not study at all that night. Plan some mild recreation or diversion; then go to bed early and get a good night's sleep.
- Get up early enough to make a leisurely trip to the place for the test – This way unforeseen events, traffic snarls, unfamiliar buildings, etc. will not upset you.
- Dress comfortably – A written test is not a fashion show. You will be known by number and not by name, so wear something comfortable.
- Leave excess paraphernalia at home – Shopping bags and odd bundles will get in your way. You need bring only the items mentioned in the official notice you received; usually everything you need is provided. Do not bring reference books to the exam. They will only confuse those last minutes and be taken away from you when in the test room.
- Arrive somewhat ahead of time – If because of transportation schedules you must get there very early, bring a newspaper or magazine to take your mind off yourself while waiting.
- Locate the examination room – When you have found the proper room, you will be directed to the seat or part of the room where you will sit. Sometimes you are given a sheet of instructions to read while you are waiting. Do not fill out any forms until you are told to do so; just read them and be prepared.
- Relax and prepare to listen to the instructions
- If you have any physical problem that may keep you from doing your best, be sure to tell the test administrator. If you are sick or in poor health, you really cannot do your best on the exam. You can come back and take the test some other time.

VII. AT THE TEST

The day of the test is here and you have the test booklet in your hand. The temptation to get going is very strong. Caution! There is more to success than knowing the right answers. You must know how to identify your papers and understand variations in the type of short-answer question used in this particular examination. Follow these suggestions for maximum results from your efforts:

1) Cooperate with the monitor

The test administrator has a duty to create a situation in which you can be as much at ease as possible. He will give instructions, tell you when to begin, check to see that you are marking your answer sheet correctly, and so on. He is not there to guard you, although he will see that your competitors do not take unfair advantage. He wants to help you do your best.

2) Listen to all instructions

Don't jump the gun! Wait until you understand all directions. In most civil service tests you get more time than you need to answer the questions. So don't be in a hurry. Read each word of instructions until you clearly understand the meaning. Study the examples, listen to all announcements and follow directions. Ask questions if you do not understand what to do.

3) Identify your papers

Civil service exams are usually identified by number only. You will be assigned a number; you must not put your name on your test papers. Be sure to copy your number correctly. Since more than one exam may be given, copy your exact examination title.

4) Plan your time

Unless you are told that a test is a "speed" or "rate of work" test, speed itself is usually not important. Time enough to answer all the questions will be provided, but this does not mean that you have all day. An overall time limit has been set. Divide the total time (in minutes) by the number of questions to determine the approximate time you have for each question.

5) Do not linger over difficult questions

If you come across a difficult question, mark it with a paper clip (useful to have along) and come back to it when you have been through the booklet. One caution if you do this – be sure to skip a number on your answer sheet as well. Check often to be sure that you have not lost your place and that you are marking in the row numbered the same as the question you are answering.

6) Read the questions

Be sure you know what the question asks! Many capable people are unsuccessful because they failed to *read* the questions correctly.

7) Answer all questions

Unless you have been instructed that a penalty will be deducted for incorrect answers, it is better to guess than to omit a question.

8) Speed tests

It is often better NOT to guess on speed tests. It has been found that on timed tests people are tempted to spend the last few seconds before time is called in marking answers at random – without even reading them – in the hope of picking up a few extra points. To discourage this practice, the instructions may warn you that your score will be "corrected" for guessing. That is, a penalty will be applied. The incorrect answers will be deducted from the correct ones, or some other penalty formula will be used.

9) Review your answers

If you finish before time is called, go back to the questions you guessed or omitted to give them further thought. Review other answers if you have time.

10) Return your test materials

If you are ready to leave before others have finished or time is called, take ALL your materials to the monitor and leave quietly. Never take any test material with you. The monitor can discover whose papers are not complete, and taking a test booklet may be grounds for disqualification.

VIII. EXAMINATION TECHNIQUES

1) Read the general instructions carefully. These are usually printed on the first page of the exam booklet. As a rule, these instructions refer to the timing of the examination; the fact that you should not start work until the signal and must stop work at a signal, etc. If there are any *special* instructions, such as a choice of questions to be answered, make sure that you note this instruction carefully.

2) When you are ready to start work on the examination, that is as soon as the signal has been given, read the instructions to each question booklet, underline any key words or phrases, such as *least*, *best*, *outline*, *describe* and the like. In this way you will tend to answer as requested rather than discover on reviewing your paper that you *listed without describing*, that you selected the *worst* choice rather than the *best* choice, etc.

3) If the examination is of the objective or multiple-choice type – that is, each question will also give a series of possible answers: A, B, C or D, and you are called upon to select the best answer and write the letter next to that answer on your answer paper – it is advisable to start answering each question in turn. There may be anywhere from 50 to 100 such questions in the three or four hours allotted and you can see how much time would be taken if you read through all the questions before beginning to answer any. Furthermore, if you come across a question or group of questions which you know would be difficult to answer, it would undoubtedly affect your handling of all the other questions.

4) If the examination is of the essay type and contains but a few questions, it is a moot point as to whether you should read all the questions before starting to answer any one. Of course, if you are given a choice – say five out of seven and the like – then it is essential to read all the questions so you can eliminate the two that are most difficult. If, however, you are asked to answer all the questions, there may be danger in trying to answer the easiest one first because you may find that you will spend too much time on it. The best technique is to answer the first question, then proceed to the second, etc.

5) Time your answers. Before the exam begins, write down the time it started, then add the time allowed for the examination and write down the time it must be completed, then divide the time available somewhat as follows:

- If 3-1/2 hours are allowed, that would be 210 minutes. If you have 80 objective-type questions, that would be an average of 2-1/2 minutes per question. Allow yourself no more than 2 minutes per question, or a total of 160 minutes, which will permit about 50 minutes to review.
- If for the time allotment of 210 minutes there are 7 essay questions to answer, that would average about 30 minutes a question. Give yourself only 25 minutes per question so that you have about 35 minutes to review.

6) The most important instruction is to *read each question* and make sure you know what is wanted. The second most important instruction is to *time yourself properly* so that you answer every question. The third most important instruction is to *answer every question.* Guess if you have to but include something for each question. Remember that you will receive no credit for a blank and will probably receive some credit if you write something in answer to an essay question. If you guess a letter – say "B" for a multiple-choice question – you may have guessed right. If you leave a blank as an answer to a multiple-choice question, the examiners may respect your feelings but it will not add a point to your score. Some exams may penalize you for wrong answers, so in such cases *only*, you may not want to guess unless you have some basis for your answer.

7) Suggestions
   a. Objective-type questions
      1. Examine the question booklet for proper sequence of pages and questions
      2. Read all instructions carefully
      3. Skip any question which seems too difficult; return to it after all other questions have been answered
      4. Apportion your time properly; do not spend too much time on any single question or group of questions
      5. Note and underline key words – *all, most, fewest, least, best, worst, same, opposite,* etc.
      6. Pay particular attention to negatives
      7. Note unusual option, e.g., unduly long, short, complex, different or similar in content to the body of the question
      8. Observe the use of "hedging" words – *probably, may, most likely,* etc.
      9. Make sure that your answer is put next to the same number as the question
      10. Do not second-guess unless you have good reason to believe the second answer is definitely more correct
      11. Cross out original answer if you decide another answer is more accurate; do not erase until you are ready to hand your paper in
      12. Answer all questions; guess unless instructed otherwise
      13. Leave time for review

   b. Essay questions
      1. Read each question carefully
      2. Determine exactly what is wanted. Underline key words or phrases.
      3. Decide on outline or paragraph answer

4. Include many different points and elements unless asked to develop any one or two points or elements
5. Show impartiality by giving pros and cons unless directed to select one side only
6. Make and write down any assumptions you find necessary to answer the questions
7. Watch your English, grammar, punctuation and choice of words
8. Time your answers; don't crowd material

8) Answering the essay question

Most essay questions can be answered by framing the specific response around several key words or ideas. Here are a few such key words or ideas:

M's: manpower, materials, methods, money, management
P's: purpose, program, policy, plan, procedure, practice, problems, pitfalls, personnel, public relations

a. Six basic steps in handling problems:
   1. Preliminary plan and background development
   2. Collect information, data and facts
   3. Analyze and interpret information, data and facts
   4. Analyze and develop solutions as well as make recommendations
   5. Prepare report and sell recommendations
   6. Install recommendations and follow up effectiveness

b. Pitfalls to avoid
   1. *Taking things for granted* – A statement of the situation does not necessarily imply that each of the elements is necessarily true; for example, a complaint may be invalid and biased so that all that can be taken for granted is that a complaint has been registered
   2. *Considering only one side of a situation* – Wherever possible, indicate several alternatives and then point out the reasons you selected the best one
   3. *Failing to indicate follow up* – Whenever your answer indicates action on your part, make certain that you will take proper follow-up action to see how successful your recommendations, procedures or actions turn out to be
   4. *Taking too long in answering any single question* – Remember to time your answers properly

IX. AFTER THE TEST

Scoring procedures differ in detail among civil service jurisdictions although the general principles are the same. Whether the papers are hand-scored or graded by machine we have described, they are nearly always graded by number. That is, the person who marks the paper knows only the number – never the name – of the applicant. Not until all the papers have been graded will they be matched with names. If other tests, such as training and experience or oral interview ratings have been given, scores will be combined. Different parts of the examination usually have different weights. For example, the written test might count 60 percent of the final grade, and a rating of training and experience 40 percent. In many jurisdictions, veterans will have a certain number of points added to their grades.

After the final grade has been determined, the names are placed in grade order and an eligible list is established. There are various methods for resolving ties between those who get the same final grade – probably the most common is to place first the name of the person whose application was received first. Job offers are made from the eligible list in the order the names appear on it. You will be notified of your grade and your rank as soon as all these computations have been made. This will be done as rapidly as possible.

People who are found to meet the requirements in the announcement are called "eligibles." Their names are put on a list of eligible candidates. An eligible's chances of getting a job depend on how high he stands on this list and how fast agencies are filling jobs from the list.

When a job is to be filled from a list of eligibles, the agency asks for the names of people on the list of eligibles for that job. When the civil service commission receives this request, it sends to the agency the names of the three people highest on this list. Or, if the job to be filled has specialized requirements, the office sends the agency the names of the top three persons who meet these requirements from the general list.

The appointing officer makes a choice from among the three people whose names were sent to him. If the selected person accepts the appointment, the names of the others are put back on the list to be considered for future openings.

That is the rule in hiring from all kinds of eligible lists, whether they are for typist, carpenter, chemist, or something else. For every vacancy, the appointing officer has his choice of any one of the top three eligibles on the list. This explains why the person whose name is on top of the list sometimes does not get an appointment when some of the persons lower on the list do. If the appointing officer chooses the second or third eligible, the No. 1 eligible does not get a job at once, but stays on the list until he is appointed or the list is terminated.

X. HOW TO PASS THE INTERVIEW TEST

The examination for which you applied requires an oral interview test. You have already taken the written test and you are now being called for the interview test – the final part of the formal examination.

You may think that it is not possible to prepare for an interview test and that there are no procedures to follow during an interview. Our purpose is to point out some things you can do in advance that will help you and some good rules to follow and pitfalls to avoid while you are being interviewed.

What is an interview supposed to test?

The written examination is designed to test the technical knowledge and competence of the candidate; the oral is designed to evaluate intangible qualities, not readily measured otherwise, and to establish a list showing the relative fitness of each candidate – as measured against his competitors – for the position sought. Scoring is not on the basis of "right" and "wrong," but on a sliding scale of values ranging from "not passable" to "outstanding." As a matter of fact, it is possible to achieve a relatively low score without a single "incorrect" answer because of evident weakness in the qualities being measured.

Occasionally, an examination may consist entirely of an oral test – either an individual or a group oral. In such cases, information is sought concerning the technical knowledges and abilities of the candidate, since there has been no written examination for this purpose. More commonly, however, an oral test is used to supplement a written examination.

Who conducts interviews?

The composition of oral boards varies among different jurisdictions. In nearly all, a representative of the personnel department serves as chairman. One of the members of the board may be a representative of the department in which the candidate would work. In some cases, "outside experts" are used, and, frequently, a businessman or some other representative of the general public is asked to serve. Labor and management or other special groups may be represented. The aim is to secure the services of experts in the appropriate field.

However the board is composed, it is a good idea (and not at all improper or unethical) to ascertain in advance of the interview who the members are and what groups they represent. When you are introduced to them, you will have some idea of their backgrounds and interests, and at least you will not stutter and stammer over their names.

What should be done before the interview?

While knowledge about the board members is useful and takes some of the surprise element out of the interview, there is other preparation which is more substantive. It *is* possible to prepare for an oral interview – in several ways:

1) Keep a copy of your application and review it carefully before the interview

This may be the only document before the oral board, and the starting point of the interview. Know what education and experience you have listed there, and the sequence and dates of all of it. Sometimes the board will ask you to review the highlights of your experience for them; you should not have to hem and haw doing it.

2) Study the class specification and the examination announcement

Usually, the oral board has one or both of these to guide them. The qualities, characteristics or knowledges required by the position sought are stated in these documents. They offer valuable clues as to the nature of the oral interview. For example, if the job involves supervisory responsibilities, the announcement will usually indicate that knowledge of modern supervisory methods and the qualifications of the candidate as a supervisor will be tested. If so, you can expect such questions, frequently in the form of a hypothetical situation which you are expected to solve. NEVER go into an oral without knowledge of the duties and responsibilities of the job you seek.

3) Think through each qualification required

Try to visualize the kind of questions you would ask if you were a board member. How well could you answer them? Try especially to appraise your own knowledge and background in each area, *measured against the job sought*, and identify any areas in which you are weak. Be critical and realistic – do not flatter yourself.

4) Do some general reading in areas in which you feel you may be weak

For example, if the job involves supervision and your past experience has NOT, some general reading in supervisory methods and practices, particularly in the field of human relations, might be useful. Do NOT study agency procedures or detailed manuals. The oral board will be testing your understanding and capacity, not your memory.

5) Get a good night's sleep and watch your general health and mental attitude

You will want a clear head at the interview. Take care of a cold or any other minor ailment, and of course, no hangovers.

What should be done on the day of the interview?

Now comes the day of the interview itself. Give yourself plenty of time to get there. Plan to arrive somewhat ahead of the scheduled time, particularly if your appointment is in the fore part of the day. If a previous candidate fails to appear, the board might be ready for you a bit early. By early afternoon an oral board is almost invariably behind schedule if there are many candidates, and you may have to wait. Take along a book or magazine to read, or your application to review, but leave any extraneous material in the waiting room when you go in for your interview. In any event, relax and compose yourself.

The matter of dress is important. The board is forming impressions about you – from your experience, your manners, your attitude, and your appearance. Give your personal appearance careful attention. Dress your best, but not your flashiest. Choose conservative, appropriate clothing, and be sure it is immaculate. This is a business interview, and your appearance should indicate that you regard it as such. Besides, being well groomed and properly dressed will help boost your confidence.

Sooner or later, someone will call your name and escort you into the interview room. *This is it.* From here on you are on your own. It is too late for any more preparation. But remember, you asked for this opportunity to prove your fitness, and you are here because your request was granted.

What happens when you go in?

The usual sequence of events will be as follows: The clerk (who is often the board stenographer) will introduce you to the chairman of the oral board, who will introduce you to the other members of the board. Acknowledge the introductions before you sit down. Do not be surprised if you find a microphone facing you or a stenotypist sitting by. Oral interviews are usually recorded in the event of an appeal or other review.

Usually the chairman of the board will open the interview by reviewing the highlights of your education and work experience from your application – primarily for the benefit of the other members of the board, as well as to get the material into the record. Do not interrupt or comment unless there is an error or significant misinterpretation; if that is the case, do not hesitate. But do not quibble about insignificant matters. Also, he will usually ask you some question about your education, experience or your present job – partly to get you to start talking and to establish the interviewing "rapport." He may start the actual questioning, or turn it over to one of the other members. Frequently, each member undertakes the questioning on a particular area, one in which he is perhaps most competent, so you can expect each member to participate in the examination. Because time is limited, you may also expect some rather abrupt switches in the direction the questioning takes, so do not be upset by it. Normally, a board member will not pursue a single line of questioning unless he discovers a particular strength or weakness.

After each member has participated, the chairman will usually ask whether any member has any further questions, then will ask you if you have anything you wish to add. Unless you are expecting this question, it may floor you. Worse, it may start you off on an extended, extemporaneous speech. The board is not usually seeking more information. The question is principally to offer you a last opportunity to present further qualifications or to indicate that you have nothing to add. So, if you feel that a significant qualification or characteristic has been overlooked, it is proper to point it out in a sentence or so. Do not compliment the board on the thoroughness of their examination – they have been sketchy, and you know it. If you wish, merely say, "No thank you, I have nothing further to add." This is a point where you can "talk yourself out" of a good impression or fail to present an important bit of information. Remember, *you close the interview yourself.*

The chairman will then say, "That is all, Mr. ______, thank you." Do not be startled; the interview is over, and quicker than you think. Thank him, gather your belongings and take your leave. Save your sigh of relief for the other side of the door.

How to put your best foot forward

Throughout this entire process, you may feel that the board individually and collectively is trying to pierce your defenses, seek out your hidden weaknesses and embarrass and confuse you. Actually, this is not true. They are obliged to make an appraisal of your qualifications for the job you are seeking, and they want to see you in your best light. Remember, they must interview all candidates and a non-cooperative candidate may become a failure in spite of their best efforts to bring out his qualifications. Here are 15 suggestions that will help you:

1) Be natural – Keep your attitude confident, not cocky

If you are not confident that you can do the job, do not expect the board to be. Do not apologize for your weaknesses, try to bring out your strong points. The board is interested in a positive, not negative, presentation. Cockiness will antagonize any board member and make him wonder if you are covering up a weakness by a false show of strength.

2) Get comfortable, but don't lounge or sprawl

Sit erectly but not stiffly. A careless posture may lead the board to conclude that you are careless in other things, or at least that you are not impressed by the importance of the occasion. Either conclusion is natural, even if incorrect. Do not fuss with your clothing, a pencil or an ashtray. Your hands may occasionally be useful to emphasize a point; do not let them become a point of distraction.

3) Do not wisecrack or make small talk

This is a serious situation, and your attitude should show that you consider it as such. Further, the time of the board is limited – they do not want to waste it, and neither should you.

4) Do not exaggerate your experience or abilities

In the first place, from information in the application or other interviews and sources, the board may know more about you than you think. Secondly, you probably will not get away with it. An experienced board is rather adept at spotting such a situation, so do not take the chance.

5) If you know a board member, do not make a point of it, yet do not hide it

Certainly you are not fooling him, and probably not the other members of the board. Do not try to take advantage of your acquaintanceship – it will probably do you little good.

6) Do not dominate the interview

Let the board do that. They will give you the clues – do not assume that you have to do all the talking. Realize that the board has a number of questions to ask you, and do not try to take up all the interview time by showing off your extensive knowledge of the answer to the first one.

7) Be attentive

You only have 20 minutes or so, and you should keep your attention at its sharpest throughout. When a member is addressing a problem or question to you, give him your undivided attention. Address your reply principally to him, but do not exclude the other board members.

8) Do not interrupt

A board member may be stating a problem for you to analyze. He will ask you a question when the time comes. Let him state the problem, and wait for the question.

9) Make sure you understand the question

Do not try to answer until you are sure what the question is. If it is not clear, restate it in your own words or ask the board member to clarify it for you. However, do not haggle about minor elements.

10) Reply promptly but not hastily

A common entry on oral board rating sheets is "candidate responded readily," or "candidate hesitated in replies." Respond as promptly and quickly as you can, but do not jump to a hasty, ill-considered answer.

11) Do not be peremptory in your answers

A brief answer is proper – but do not fire your answer back. That is a losing game from your point of view. The board member can probably ask questions much faster than you can answer them.

12) Do not try to create the answer you think the board member wants

He is interested in what kind of mind you have and how it works – not in playing games. Furthermore, he can usually spot this practice and will actually grade you down on it.

13) Do not switch sides in your reply merely to agree with a board member

Frequently, a member will take a contrary position merely to draw you out and to see if you are willing and able to defend your point of view. Do not start a debate, yet do not surrender a good position. If a position is worth taking, it is worth defending.

14) Do not be afraid to admit an error in judgment if you are shown to be wrong

The board knows that you are forced to reply without any opportunity for careful consideration. Your answer may be demonstrably wrong. If so, admit it and get on with the interview.

15) Do not dwell at length on your present job

The opening question may relate to your present assignment. Answer the question but do not go into an extended discussion. You are being examined for a *new* job, not your present one. As a matter of fact, try to phrase ALL your answers in terms of the job for which you are being examined.

Basis of Rating

Probably you will forget most of these "do's" and "don'ts" when you walk into the oral interview room. Even remembering them all will not ensure you a passing grade. Perhaps you did not have the qualifications in the first place. But remembering them will help you to put your best foot forward, without treading on the toes of the board members.

Rumor and popular opinion to the contrary notwithstanding, an oral board wants you to make the best appearance possible. They know you are under pressure – but they also want to see how you respond to it as a guide to what your reaction would be under the pressures of the job you seek. They will be influenced by the degree of poise you display, the personal traits you show and the manner in which you respond.

ABOUT THIS BOOK

This book contains tests divided into Examination Sections. Go through each test, answering every question in the margin. At the end of each test look at the answer key and check your answers. On the ones you got wrong, look at the right answer choice and learn. Do not fill in the answers first. Do not memorize the questions and answers, but understand the answer and principles involved. On your test, the questions will likely be different from the samples. Questions are changed and new ones added. If you understand these past questions you should have success with any changes that arise. Tests may consist of several types of questions. We have additional books on each subject should more study be advisable or necessary for you. Finally, the more you study, the better prepared you will be. This book is intended to be the last thing you study before you walk into the examination room. Prior study of relevant texts is also recommended. NLC publishes some of these in our Fundamental Series. Knowledge and good sense are important factors in passing your exam. Good luck also helps. So now study this Passbook, absorb the material contained within and take that knowledge into the examination. Then do your best to pass that exam.

EXAMINATION SECTION

EXAMINATION SECTION
TEST 1

DIRECTIONS: Each question or incomplete statement is followed by several suggested answers or completions. Select the one that BEST answers the question or completes the statement. *PRINT THE LETTER OF THE CORRECT ANSWER IN THE SPACE AT THE RIGHT.*

1. The reliability of information obtained increases with the number of persons interviewed. The more the interviewees differ in their statements, the more persons it is necessary to interview to ascertain the true facts. 1.____
According to this statement, the dependability of the information about an occurrence obtained from interviews is related to

   A. how many people are interviewed
   B. how soon after the occurrence an interview can be arranged
   C. the individual technique of the interviewer
   D. the interviewer's ability to detect differences in the statements of interviewees

2. A sufficient quantity of the material supplied as evidence enables the laboratory expert to determine the true nature of the substance, whereas an extremely limited specimen may be an abnormal sample containing foreign matter not indicative of the true nature of the material. 2.____
On the basis of this statement alone, it may be concluded that a reason for giving an adequate sample of material for evidence to a laboratory expert is that

   A. a limited specimen spoils more quickly than a larger sample
   B. a small sample may not truly represent the evidence
   C. he cannot analyze a small sample correctly
   D. he must have enough material to keep a part of it untouched to show in court

Questions 3-4.

DIRECTIONS: Questions 3 and 4 are based ONLY on the information given in the following paragraph.

Credibility of a witness is usually governed by his character and is evidenced by his reputation for truthfulness. Personal or financial reasons or a criminal record may cause a witness to give false information to avoid being implicated. Age, sex, physical and mental abnormalities, loyalty, revenge, social and economic status, indulgence in alcohol, and the influence of other persons are some of the many factors which may affect the accuracy, willingness, or ability with which witnesses observe, interpret, and describe occurrences.

3. According to the above paragraph, a witness may, for personal reasons, give wrong information about an occurrence because he 3.____

   A. wants to protect his reputation for truthfulness
   B. wants to embarrass the investigator
   C. doesn't want to become involved
   D. doesn't really remember what happened

4. According to the above paragraph, factors which influence the witness of an occurrence may affect 4.____

   A. not only what he tells about it, but what he was able and wanted to see of it
   B. only what he describes and interprets later but not what he actually sees at the time of the event
   C. what he sees but not what he describes
   D. what he is willing to see but not what he is able to see

5. There are few individuals or organizations on whom some records are not kept. This sentence means MOST NEARLY that 5.____

   A. a few organizations keep most of the records on individuals
   B. some of the records on a few individuals are destroyed and not kept
   C. there are few records kept on individuals
   D. there is some kind of record kept on almost every individual

Questions 6-10.

DIRECTIONS: Questions 6 through 10 are based SOLELY on the following paragraph.

Those statutes of limitations which are of interest to a claim examiner are the ones affecting third party actions brought against an insured covered by a liability policy of insurance. Such statutes of limitations are legislative enactments limiting the time within which such actions at law may be brought. Research shows that such periods differ from state to state and vary within the states with the type of action brought. The laws of the jurisdiction in which the action is brought govern and determine the period within which the action may be instituted, regardless of the place of the cause of action or the residence of the parties at the time of cause of action. The period of time set by a statute of limitations for a tort action starts from the moment the alleged tort is committed. The period usually extends continuously until its expiration, upon which legal action may no longer be brought. However, there is a suspension of the running of the period when a defendant has concealed himself in order to avoid service of legal process. The suspension continues until the defendant discontinues his concealment and then the period starts running again. A defendant may, by his agreement or conduct, be legally barred from asserting the statute of limitations as a defense to an action. The insurance carrier for the defendant may, by the misrepresentation of the claims man, cause such a bar against use of the statute of limitations by the defendant. If the claim examiner of the insurance carrier has by his conduct or assertion lulled the plaintiff into a false sense of security by false representations, the defendant may be barred from setting up the statute of limitations as a defense.

6. Of the following, the MOST suitable title for the above paragraph is 6.____

   A. Fraudulent Use of the Statute of Limitations
   B. Parties at Interest in a Lawsuit
   C. The Claim Examiner and the Law
   D. The Statute of Limitations in Claims Work

7. The period of time during which a third party action may be brought against an insured covered by a liability policy depends on 7.____

   A. the laws of the jurisdiction in which the action is brought
   B. where the cause of action which is the subject of the suit took place
   C. where the claimant lived at the time of the cause of action
   D. where the insured lived at the time of the cause of action

8. Time limits in third party actions which are set by the statutes of limitations described above are 8.____

   A. determined by claimant's place of residence at start of action
   B. different in a state for different actions
   C. the same from state to state for the same type of action
   D. the same within a state regardless of type of action

9. According to the above paragraph, grounds which may be legally used to prevent a defendant from using the statute of limitations as a defense in the action described are 9.____

   A. defendant's agreement or concealment; a charge of liability for death and injury
   B. defendant's agreement or conduct; misrepresentation by the claims man
   C. fraudulent concealment by claim examiner; a charge of liability for death or injury; defendant's agreement
   D. misrepresentation by claim examiner of carrier; defendant's agreement; plaintiff's concealment

10. Suppose an alleged tort was committed on January 1, 2013 and that the period in which action may be taken is set at three years by the statute of limitations. Suppose further that the defendant, in order to avoid service of legal process, had concealed himself from July 1, 2015 through December 31, 2015.
In this case, the defendant may NOT use the statute of limitations as a defense unless action is brought by the plaintiff after 10.____

   A. January 1, 2016
   B. February 28, 2016
   C. June 30, 2016
   D. August 1, 2016

Questions 11-15.

DIRECTIONS: Questions 11 through 15 are based SOLELY on the information given in the following paragraph.

The nature of the interview varies with the aim or the use to which it is put. While these uses vary widely, interviews are basically of three types: fact-finding, informing, and motivating. One of these purposes usually predominates in an interview, but not the exclusion of the other two. If the main purpose is fact-finding, for example, the interviewer must often motivate the interviewee to cooperate in revealing the facts. A major factor in the interview is the interaction of the personalities of the interviewer and the interviewee. The interviewee may not wish to reveal the facts sought, or even though willing enough to impart them, he may not be able to do so because of a lack of clear understanding as to what is wanted or because of lack of ability to put into words the information he has to give. On the other hand, the interviewer may not be able to grasp and report accurately the facts which the one being interviewed is trying to convey. Also, the interviewer's prejudice may make him not want to get at the real facts or make him unable to recognize the truth.

11. According to the above paragraph, the purpose of an interview 11._____

A. determines the nature of the interview
B. is usually the same for the three basic types of interviews
C. is predominantly motivation of the interviewee
D. is usually to check on the accuracy of facts previously obtained

12. In discussing the use or purpose of an interview, the above paragraph points out that 12._____

A. a good interview should have only one purpose
B. an interview usually has several uses that are equally important
C. fact-finding should be the main purpose of an interview
D. the interview usually has one main purpose

13. According to the above paragraph, an obstacle to the successful interview sometimes attributable to the interviewee is 13._____

A. a lack of understanding of how to conduct an interview
B. an inability to express himself
C. prejudice toward the interviewer
D. too great a desire to please

14. According to the above paragraph, one way in which the interviewer may help the interviewee to reveal the facts sought is to 14._____

A. make him willing to impart the facts by stating clearly the consequences of false information
B. make sure he understands what information is wanted
C. motivate him by telling him how important he is in the investigation
D. tell him what words to use to convey the information wanted

15. According to the above paragraph, bias on the part of the interviewer could 15._____

A. be due to inability to understand the facts being imparted
B. lead him to report the facts accurately
C. make the interviewee unwilling to impart the truth
D. prevent him from determining the facts

Questions 16-20.

DIRECTIONS: Questions 16 through 20 are to be based SOLELY on the information given in the following paragraph.

PROCEDURE TO OBTAIN REIMBURSEMENT FROM DEPARTMENT OF HEALTH FOR CARE OF PHYSICALLY HANDICAPPED CHILDREN

Application for reimbursement must be received by the Department of Health within 30 days of the date of hospital admission in order that the Department of Hospitals may be reimbursed from the date of admission. Upon determination that the patient is physically handicapped, as defined under Chapter 780 of the State Laws, the ward clerk shall prepare seven copies of Department of Health Form A-1 or A-2 "Application and Authorization," and shall submit six copies to the institutional Collections Unit. The ward clerk shall also initiate two copies of Department of Health Form B-1 or B-2 "Financial and Social Report," and shall for-

ward them to the institutional Collections Unit for completion of page 1 and routing to the Social Service Division for completion of the Social Summary on page 2. Social Service Division shall return Form B-1 or B-2 to the institutional Collections Unit, which shall forward one copy of Form B-1 or B-2 and six copies of Form A-1 or A-2 to Central Office Division of Collections for transmission to Bureau of Handicapped Children, Department of Health.

16. According to the above paragraph, the Department of Health will pay for hospital care for 16.____

    A. children who are physically handicapped
    B. any children who are ward patients
    C. physically handicapped adults and children
    D. thirty days for eligible children

17. According to the procedure described in the above paragraph, the definition of what constitutes a physical handicap is made by the 17.____

    A. attending physician
    B. laws of the state
    C. Social Service Division
    D. ward clerk

18. According to the above paragraph, Form B-1 or B-2 is 18.____

    A. a three page form containing detachable pages
    B. an authorization form issued by the Department of Hospitals
    C. completed by the ward clerk after the Social Summary has been entered
    D. sent to the institutional Collections Unit by the Social Service Division

19. According to the above paragraph, after their return by the Social Service Division, the institutional Collections Unit keeps 19.____

    A. one copy of Form A-1 or A-2
    B. one copy of Form A-1 or A-2 and one copy of Form B-1 or B-2
    C. one copy of Form B-1 or B-2
    D. no copies of Forms A-1 or A-2 or B-1 or B-2

20. According to the above paragraph, forwarding the "Application and Authorization" to the Department of Health is the responsibility of the 20.____

    A. Bureau for Handicapped Children
    B. Central Office Division of Collections
    C. Institutional Collections Unit
    D. Social Service Division

21. An investigator interviews members of the public at his desk. 21.____
    The attitude of the public toward this department will probably be LEAST affected by this investigator's

    A. courtesy
    B. efficiency
    C. height
    D. neatness

22. While you are conducting an interview, the telephone on your desk rings. 22.____
    Of the following, it would be BEST for you to

    A. ask the interviewer at the next desk to answer your telephone and take the message for you
    B. excuse yourself, pick up the telephone, and tell the person on the other end you are busy and will call him back later

C. ignore the ringing telephone and continue with the interview
D. use another telephone to inform the operator not to put calls through to you while you are conducting an interview

23. An interviewee is at your desk, which is quite near to desks where other people work. He beckons you a little closer and starts to talk in a low voice as though he does not want anyone else to hear him. 23.____
Under these circumstances, the BEST thing for you to do is to

A. ask him to speak a little louder so that he can be heard
B. cut the interview short and not get involved in his problems
C. explain that people at other desks are not eavesdroppers
D. listen carefully to what he says and give it consideration

24. In the course of your work, you have developed a good relationship with the clerk in charge of the information section of a certain government agency from which you must frequently obtain information. This agency's procedures require that a number of long complicated forms be prepared by you before the information can be released. 24.____
For you to ask the clerk in charge to release information to you without your presenting the forms would be

A. *unwise* mainly because the information so obtained is no longer considered official
B. *wise* mainly because a great deal of time will be saved by you and by the clerk
C. *unwise* mainly because it may impair the good relations you have established
D. *wise* mainly because more information can usually be obtained through friendly contacts

25. Sometimes city employees are offered gifts by members of the public in an effort to show appreciation for acts performed purely as a matter of duty. An investigator to whom such a gift was offered refused to accept it. 25.____
The action of the investigator was

A. *bad;* the gift should have been accepted to avoid being rude to the person making the offer
B. *bad;* salaries paid city employees are not high enough to justify such refusals
C. *good;* he should accept such a gift only when he has done a special favor for someone
D. *good;* the acceptance of such gifts may raise doubts as to the honesty of the employee

26. From the point of view of current correct English usage and grammar, the MOST acceptable of the following sentences is: 26.____

A. Each claimant was allowed the full amount of their medical expenses,
B. Either of the three witnesses is available
C. Every one of the witnesses was asked to tell his story
D. Neither of the witnesses are right

27. From the point of view of current correct English usage and grammar, the MOST acceptable of the following sentences is: 27.____

A. Beside the statement to the police, the witness spoke to no one
B. He made no statement other than to the police and I

C. He made no statement to any one else, aside from the police
D. The witness spoke to no one but me

28. From the point of view of current correct English usage and grammar, the MOST acceptable of the following sentences is: 28.____

A. The claimant has no one to blame but himself
B. The boss sent us, he and I, to deliver the packages
C. The lights come from mine and not his car
D. There was room on the stairs for him and myself

29. Of the following excerpts selected from letters, the one which is considered by modern letter writing experts to be the BEST is: 29.____

A. Attached please find the application form to be filled out by you. Return the form to this office at the above address.
B. Forward to this office your check accompanied by the application form enclosed with this letter
C. If you wish to apply, please complete and return the enclosed form with your check
D. In reply to your letter of December ______, enclosed herewith please find the application form you requested

30. Which of the following sentences would be MOST acceptable, from the point of view of current correct English usage and grammar, in a letter answering a request for information about eligibility for clinic care? 30.____

A. Admission to this clinic is limited to patients' inability to pay for medical care.
B. Patients who can pay little or nothing for medical care are treated in this clinic.
C. The patient's ability to pay for medical care is the determining factor in his admissibility to this clinic.
D. This clinic is for the patient's that cannot afford to pay or that can pay a little for medical care.

31. A city employee who writes a letter requesting information from a business man should realize that, of the following, it is MOST important to 31.____

A. end the letter with a polite closing
B. make the letter short enough to fit on one page
C. use a form, such as a questionnaire, to save the businessman's time
D. use a courteous tone that will get the desired cooperation

Questions 32-35.

DIRECTIONS: Each of Questions 32 through 35 consists of a sentence which may be classified appropriately under one of the following four categories:

A. incorrect because of faulty grammar or sentence structure
B. incorrect because of faulty punctuation
C. incorrect because of faulty capitalization
D. correct

Examine each sentence carefully. Then, in the space at the right, print the letter preceding the category which is the BEST of the four suggested above. Each incorrect sentence contains only one type of error. Consider a sentence correct if it contains none of the types of errors mentioned, although there may be other correct ways of expressing the same thought.

32. Despite the efforts of the Supervising mechanic, the elevator could not be started. 32.____

33. The U.S. Weather Bureau, weather record for the accident date was checked. 33.____

34. John Jones accidentally pushed the wrong button and then all the lights went out. 34.____

35. The investigator ought to of had the witness sign the statement. 35.____

Questions 36-45.

DIRECTIONS: Each of Questions 36 to 45 consists of a capitalized word followed by four suggested meanings of the word. For each question, choose the word or phrase which means MOST NEARLY the same as the word in capital letters.

36. ABUT 36.____

A. abandon B. assist C. border on D. renounce

37. ABSCOND 37.____

A. draw in
B. give up
C. refrain from
D. steal off

38. BEQUEATH 38.____

A. deaden B. hand down C. make sad D. scold

39. BOGUS 39.____

A. sad B. false C. shocking D. stolen

40. CALAMITY 40.____

A. disaster B. female C. insanity D. patriot

41. COMPULSORY 41.____

A. binding B. ordinary C. protected D. ruling

42. CONSIGN 42.____

A. agree with B. benefit C. commit D. drive down

43. DEBILITY 43.____

A. failure B. legality C. quality D. weakness

44. DEFRAUD 44.____

A. cheat B. deny C. reveal D. tie

45. DEPOSITION 45.____

A. absence B. publication C. removal D. testimony

KEY (CORRECT ANSWERS)

1. A	11. A	21. C	31. D	41. A
2. B	12. D	22. B	32. C	42. C
3. C	13. B	23. D	33. B	43. D
4. A	14. B	24. C	34. D	44. A
5. D	15. D	25. D	35. A	45. D
6. D	16. A	26. C	36. C	
7. A	17. B	27. D	37. D	
8. B	18. D	28. A	38. B	
9. B	19. C	29. C	39. B	
10. C	20. B	30. B	40. A	

TEST 2

Questions 1-10.

DIRECTIONS: Each of Questions 1 to 10 consists of a capitalized word followed by four suggested meanings of the word. For each question, choose the word or phrase which means MOST NEARLY the same as the word in capital letters.

1. DOMICILE 1.____
   A. anger B. dwelling C. tame D. willing

2. HEARSAY 2.____
   A. selfish B. serious C. rumor D. unlikely

3. HOMOGENEOUS 3.____
   A. human B. racial C. similar D. unwise

4. ILLICIT 4.____
   A. understood B. uneven C. unkind D. unlawful

5. LEDGER 5.____
   A. book of accounts B. editor
   C. periodical D. shelf

6. NARRATIVE 6.____
   A. gossip B. natural C. negative D. story

7. PLAUSIBLE 7.____
   A. reasonable B. respectful
   C. responsible D. rightful

8. RECIPIENT 8.____
   A. absentee B. receiver C. speaker D. substitute

9. SUBSTANTIATE 9.____
   A. appear for B. arrange C. confirm D. combine

10. SURMISE 10.____
   A. aim B. break C. guess D. order

Questions 11-14.

DIRECTIONS: In Questions 11 to 14, one of the four words is misspelled. For each question, choose the word which is misspelled.

11. A. absence B. accummulate 11.____
   C. acknowledgment D. audible

12. A. benificiary B. disbursement C. exorbitant D. incidentally 12.____

13. A. inoculate B. liaison C. acquire D. noticable 13.____

14. A. peddler B. permissible C. persuade D. pertenant 14.____

15. A. reconciliation B. responsable C. sizable D. substantial 15.____

16. Suppose a badly cracked sidewalk, 160 feet long and 14 feet wide, is to be torn up and replaced in four equal sections.
Each section will measure ______ square feet. 16.____

A. 40 B. 220 C. 560 D. 680

17. A businessman pays R dollars a month in rent, has a weekly payroll of P dollars, and a utility bill of U dollars for each two months.
His annual expenses can be expressed by 17.____

A. 12(R+P+U)
B. 52(R+P+U)
C. 12(R+52P+6U)
D. 12(R+4P+2U)

18. An interviewer can interview P number of people in H number of hours, including the time needed to prepare a report on each interview.
The number of people he can interview in a work week of W hours is represented by 18.____

A. $\frac{HW}{P}$ B. $\frac{PW}{H}$ C. $\frac{PH}{W}$ D. $\frac{35H}{P}$

19. Claims investigated by a certain unit total $8,430,000 for the year.
If the cost of investigating these claims is 17.3 cents per $100, the yearly cost of investigating these claims is MOST NEARLY 19.____

A. $1,450 B. $14,500 C. $145,000 D. $1,450,000

20. Suppose that a business you are investigating presents the following figures: 20.____

Year	Net Income	Tax Rate on Net Income
1994	$55,000	20%
1995	55,000	30%
1996	65,000	20%
1997	52,000	25%
1998	62,000	30%
1999	68,000	25%

According to these figures, it is MOST accurate to say that 20.____

A. less tax was due in 1998 than in 1999
B. more tax was due in 1994 than in 1997
C. the same amount of tax was due in 1994 and 1995
D. the same amount of tax was due in 1996 and 1997

21. In 1996, the number of investigations completed in a certain unit had increased 230 over the number completed in 1995, an increase of 10%. In 1997, the number completed decreased 10% from the number completed in 1996. 21.____
Therefore, the number of investigations completed in 1997 was ______ the number completed in 1995.

A. 23 less than
B. 123 less than
C. 230 more than
D. the same as

22. Assume that during a certain period Unit A investigated 400 cases and Unit B investigated 300 cases. 22.____
If each unit doubled its number of investigations, the proportion of Unit A's investigations to Unit B's investigations would then be ______ it was.

A. twice what
B. one-half as large as
C. one-third larger than
D. the same as

23. In a certain family, the teenage daughter's annual earnings are 5/8 the earnings of her brother and 1/5 the earnings of her father. 23.____
If her brother earns $19,200 a year, then her father's annual earnings are

A. $60,000 B. $75,000 C. $80,000 D. $96,000

24. Assume that of the 1,700 verifications made by a certain investigating unit in a one week period, 40% were birth records, 30% were military records, 10% were citizenship records, and the remainder were miscellaneous records. Then the MOST accurate of the following statements about the relative number of different records is that 24.____

A. citizenship records verifications equaled 20% of military record verifications
B. fewer than 700 verifications were birth records
C. miscellaneous records verifications were 20% more than citizenship records verifications
D. more than 550 verifications were military records

25. Two units, A and B, answer, respectively, 1,000 and 1,500 inquiries a month. 25.____
Assuming that the number of inquiries answered by Unit A increase at the rate of 20 each month, while those answered by Unit B decrease at the rate of 5 each month, the two units will answer the same number of inquiries at the end of ______ months.

A. 10 B. 15 C. 20 D. 25

26. For the claim examiner to obtain a signed statement the very first time he interviews a witness to an accident is USUALLY 26.____

A. *bad;* the witness should be given more time in which to recall the details of the accident
B. *good;* delay might result in the witness forgetting details
C. *good;* no further appointments with the witness would then be needed
D. *good;* the story given by this witness would then be the first description of the accident

Questions 27-30.

DIRECTIONS: Questions 27 to 30 are based on the following description by a physician of the injuries sustained by the victim of an accident.

Compound fracture of the right humerus. Contusions and ecchymoses of the right chest. Four-inch long laceration on the dorsal surface of the right hand.

27. According to this description, the victim has a broken 27.____

A. ankle B. arm C. knee D. thigh

28. The broken bone is 28.____

A. broken in more than one place
B. crushed
C. protruding through the skin
D. splintered

29. Contusions are 29.____

A. bruises
B. skin scrapes or cuts
C. swellings
D. torn muscles

30. The laceration of the right hand is on the 30.____

A. back of the hand
B. little finger side
C. palm
D. thumb side

31. Suppose a claim examiner desires to obtain a signed statement during an appointment in a witness's home. He finds that the witness is cooperative, but has a large family whose members stay with him in the living room, talking and looking at television. After considering the problem of getting the signed statement, the claim examiner should 31.____

A. leave after making another appointment since his visit is an intrusion at this time
B. suggest that he and the witness use another room where they can give the statement their full attention
C. take advantage of the friendly atmosphere in the living room by having the statement drawn up and signed there
D. tell the witness to get his family to stop talking and to turn off the television set so that he and the witness can concentrate

32. Claim examiners occasionally expose fake automobile injury claims in which bruises and lacerations from falls, barroom brawls, or other mishaps are attributed to an insured commercial vehicle. 32.____
Since the claimant usually tries to pick a situation in which the driver is likely to be unaware of the accident and so can not contradict the claim, which of the following is MOST likely to be the claimant's story?

A. The front end of a truck with defective brake struck him and the truck kept going.
B. The front end of a truck sideswiped him as the driver backed into a parking space.
C. A truck knocked him over while backing into a loading space.
D. The rear end of a truck making a sharp turn struck him.

33. Suppose there is a rule in your office that signed statements of claimants should be witnessed by a person who has no direct interest in the claim. 33.____
In accordance with this rule, when a claimant is willing to sign a statement in his home, it would be BEST for you to have the claimant's signature witnessed by

A. a neighbor
B. his attorney
C. his wife
D. yourself

34. The attitude presented by the claim examiner to the claimant should ALWAYS leave the claimant with the feeling that 34.____

A. he will be treated fairly
B. he will receive damages
C. his claim has no basis
D. the claim examiner is his friend

35. If a claimant states that his vision has been impaired by an accident, it would be BEST to have him examined by a physician who is a specialist in 35.____

A. dermatology
B. opthalmology
C. otology
D. urology

36. Suppose that witness W tells you, the claim examiner, that Mr. X also witnessed the accident you are investigating. Mr. X denies that he has any knowledge of the accident. For you to have Mr. X sign a statement that he has no knowledge of the accident is wise MAINLY because such a statement 36.____

A. casts doubt on Mr. X's reliability if he should be a surprise witness for the opposition
B. makes it unnecessary for you to further investigate Mr. X
C. proves that Mr. X is telling the truth
D. proves that the statements made by witness W are unreliable and should be investigated further

37. A claim examiner admitted that the settlement negotiations were not progressing because of a clash of personalities and suggested that another claim examiner continue the negotiations. 37.____
Such an action by the claim examiner is

A. *sensible;* it reduces his responsibility if the settlement negotiations fail
B. *foolish;* it is an admission that he has an irritating personality and can not get along with people
C. *sensible;* it shows he recognizes the problem and a possible method of completing the settlement
D. *foolish;* it gives the claimant an advantage in the negotiations

38. In evaluating a doctor's fitness to serve as an expert witness in a negligence case, the claim examiner should give FIRST consideration to the doctor's 38.____

A. field of specialization
B. previous total experience as a witness in negligence cases
C. standing in the community and in his profession
D. total formal schooling

39. A claim examiner, showing his identification, introduced himself to a housewife by saying, *I am Mr. Nichols from the Department of... We are trying to get information about an accident which occurred in front of your house.* 39.____
The claim examiner's approach was

A. *good;* by identifying himself and stating his purpose, he is apt to get better cooperation
B. *good;* by giving his name, he puts the interview on a non-personal basis
C. *poor;* by revealing his purpose immediately, he may lose the woman's cooperation because of fear
D. *poor;* he should stress the importance of cooperating with city departments

40. Witness A describes an individual as being *of medium height.* Witness B describes the same individual as being *tall and thin.* 40.____
To clear up this difference in description of the individual's height, it would be BEST for you to

A. ask another witness to describe the individual
B. ask both witnesses to compare the individual's height with that of a person of known height
C. average the difference and describe the individual as being *medium tall*
D. check both witnesses' judgment on other factors to decide which witness is more reliable

41. A claimant against the city is in the hospital as the result of an automobile accident. An interview with this claimant might eliminate confusion caused by contradictory statements of witnesses to the accident. 41.____
Under these circumstances, the BEST action for the claim examiner assigned to the case to take FIRST is to

A. determine whether the claimant is in a condition that would permit an interview
B. postpone interviewing the claimant until he leaves the hospital
C. try to resolve the problem by re-examining the witnesses whose statements are in conflict
D. try to get an immediate short interview in case the person should die

42. The claimant is an occupant of a building, ownership of which was taken over by the city one day before his accident. He has bruises and contusions which he attributes to tripping on a loose board on a stairway. Several tenants state that they had complained many times to the previous owner of the building about the same loose board. 42.____
Which of the following would tend MOST to suggest fraudulent intent on the part of the claimant?

A. The claimant is represented by an insurance company with which he holds a policy covering this type of accident.
B. The claimant is the previous owner of the building, and there are no witnesses to the accident.
C. It is established by reliable witnesses that the claimant tripped over the loose board while intoxicated.
D. Witnesses state that the claimant tripped over the loose board while chasing a stray dog down the stairway.

43. At the request of the investigator, witness A added a signed paragraph to a statement already signed by witness B while witness B was present. This paragraph stated that witness A's version of the accident was exactly the same as that of witness B. Authorities in the field of claim examining would GENERALLY consider the addition of such a paragraph as 43.____

A. *good;* it makes the statement of witness B more believable
B. *bad;* witness A should have been asked to add his statement after witness B had left
C. *good;* the effect is to make both witnesses more cooperative
D. *bad;* since witnesses rarely give identical versions of an accident, the validity of this additional statement would be questioned

44. The train operator's statement was that he had applied brakes immediately on seeing the man collapse and fall onto the tracks, but he could not stop soon enough and ran over him. If proving absence of negligence in this case depends entirely on showing that the accident was beyond the train operator's control, which, of the following circumstances would, by itself, show that there was no negligence? 44.____

A. Five witnesses agreed independently that the man had apparently collapsed from a heart attack.
B. Five witnesses agreed independently that the train was traveling at a speed which was far under the normal approach speed.
C. The train operator's record showed that he had been involved in no previous accident although employed thirty years as a train operator.
D. At the moment the man fell, the distance between him and the train was less than the minimum distance at which the train could stop at normal approach speed.

45. No proper evaluation of a claim can be made without a working knowledge of the law of the jurisdiction in which an accident occurred. Of the following, the CHIEF implication of this statement is that 45.____

A. claims are based on where the accident occurred
B. evaluation of the law is a proper function of the claim examiner
C. local laws affect the claim examiner's decisions
D. the best claim examiners are attorneys

KEY (CORRECT ANSWERS)

1. B	11. B	21. A	31. B	41. A
2. C	12. A	22. D	32. D	42. B
3. C	13. D	23. A	33. A	43. D
4. D	14. D	24. B	34. A	44. D
5. A	15. B	25. C	35. B	45. C
6. D	16. C	26. B	36. A	
7. A	17. C	27. B	37. C	
8. B	18. B	28. C	38. A	
9. C	19. B	29. A	39. A	
10. C	20. D	30. A	40. B	

EXAMINATION SECTION

TEST 1

DIRECTIONS: Each question or incomplete statement is followed by several suggested answers or completions. Select the one that BEST answers the question or completes the statement. *PRINT THE LETTER OF THE CORRECT ANSWER IN THE SPACE AT THE RIGHT.*

1. An investigator uses Forms A, B, and C in filling out his investigation reports. He uses Form B five times as often as Form A, and he uses Form C three times as often as Form B. 1.____
   If the total number of all forms used by the investigator in a month equal 735, how many times was Form B used?
   A. 150 B. 175 C. 205 D. 235

2. Of all the investigators in one agency, 25% work in a particular building. Of these, 12% have desks on the 14th floor. 2.____
   What percentage of the investigators work in this building but do NOT have desks on the 14th floor?
   A. 12% B. 13% C. 22% D. 23%

3. An investigator is given two reports to read. Report P is 160 pages long and takes the investigator 3 hours and 20 minutes to read. 3.____
   If Report S is 254 pages long and the investigator reads it at the same rate as he reads Report P, how long will it take him to read Report S? _____ hours _____ minutes.
   A. 4; 15 B. 4; 50 C. 5; 10 D. 5; 30

4. A team of 6 investigators was assigned to interview 234 people. 4.____
   If half the investigators conduct twice as many interviews as the other half, and the slow group interviews 12 persons a day, how many days would it take to complete this assignment? _____ days.
   A. 4½ B. 5 C. 6 D. 6½

5. The investigators in one agency conduct an average of 12 interviews an hour from 10 A.M. to 12 noon and from 1 P.M. to 5 P.M. daily. The director of his agency knows from past experience that 20% of those called in to be interviewed are unable to keep the appointments that were scheduled. 5.____
   If the director wants his staff to be kept occupied with interviews for the entire time period that has been set aside for this function, how many appointments should be scheduled for each day?
   A. 86 B. 90 C. 96 D. 101

6. An investigator has a 430-page report to read. The first day, he is able to read 20 pages. The second day, he reads 10 pages more than the first day, and the third day, he reads 15 pages more than the second day. 6.____

If, on the following days, he continues to read at the same rate as he was reading on the third day, he will complete the report on the _____ day.
A. 7th B. 8th C. 10th D. 11th

7. The 36 investigators in an agency are each required to submit 25 investigation reports a week. These reports are filled out on a certain form, and only one copy of the form is needed per report. 7.____
Allowing 20% for waste, how many packages of 45 forms a piece should be ordered for each weekly period?
A. 15 B. 20 C. 25 D. 30

8. During the fiscal year, an investigative unit received $260 for stationery and telephone expenditures. It spent 43% for stationery and 1/3 of the balance for telephone service. 8.____
The amount of money that was left at the end of the fiscal year was MOST NEARLY
A. $49 B. $50 C. $99 D. $109

Questions 9-10.

DIRECTIONS: Questions 9 and 10 are to be answered SOLELY on the data given below.

Number of days absent per worker (sickness)	1	2	3	4	5	6	7	8 or Over
Number of Workers	96	45	16	3	1	0	1	0

Total Number of Workers: 500

9. The TOTAL number of man days lost due to illness in 2020 was 9.____
A. 137 B. 154 C. 162 D. 258

10. Of the 500 workers studied, the number who lost NO days due to sickness in 2020 was 10.____
A. 230 B. 298 C. 338 D. 372

Questions 11-13.

DIRECTIONS: Questions 11 through 13 are to be answered SOLELY on the basis of the following passage.

The rise of urban-industrial society has complicated the social arrangements needed to regulate contacts between people. As a consequence, there has been an unprecedented increase in the volume of laws and regulations designed to control individual conduct and to govern the relationship of the individual to others. In a century, there has been an eight-fold increase in the crimes for which one may be prosecuted.

For these offenses, the courts have the ultimate responsibility for redressing wrongs and convicting the guilty. The body of legal precepts gives the impression of an abstract and evenhanded dispensation of justice. Actually, the personnel of the agencies applying these precepts are faced with the difficulties of fitting abstract principles to highly variable situations emerging from the dynamics of everyday life. It is inevitable that discrepancies should exist between precept and practice.

The legal institutions serve as a framework for the social order by their slowness to respond to the caprices of transitory fad. This valuable contribution exacts a price in terms of the inflexibility of legal institutions in responding to new circumstances. This possibility is promoted by the changes in values and norms of the dynamic larger culture of which the legal precepts are a part.

11. According to the above passage, the increase in the number of laws and regulations during the twentieth century can be attributed to the — 11.____
    A. complexity of modern industrial society
    B. increased seriousness of offenses committed
    C. growth of individualism
    D. anonymity of urban living

12. According to the above passage, which of the following presents a problem to the staff of legal agencies? The — 12.____
    A. need to eliminate the discrepancy between precept and practice
    B. necessity to apply abstract legal precepts to rapidly changing conditions
    C. responsibility for reducing the number of abstract legal principles
    D. responsibility for understanding offenses in terms of the real-life situations from which they emerge

13. According to the above passage, it can be concluded that legal institutions affect social institutions by — 13.____
    A. preventing change
    B. keeping pace with its norms and values
    C. changing its norms and values
    D. providing stability

Questions 14-16.

DIRECTIONS: Questions 14 through 16 are to be answered SOLELY on the basis of information given in the following passage.

A personnel interviewer, selecting job applicants, may find that he reacts badly to some people even on first contact. This reaction cannot usually be explained by things that the interviewee has done or said. Most of us have had the experience of liking or disliking, of feeling comfortable and uncomfortable with people on first acquaintance, long before we have had a chance to make a conscious, rational decision about them. Often, too, our liking or disliking is transmitted to the other person by subtle processes such as gestures, posture, voice intonations, or choice of words. The point to be kept in mind is this: the relations between people are complex and occur at several levels, from the conscious to the unconscious. This is true whether the relationship is brief or long, formal or informal.

Some of the major dynamics of personality which operate on the unconscious level are projection, sublimation, rationalization, and repression. Encountering these for the first time, one is apt to think of them as representing pathological states. In the extreme, they undoubtedly are, but they exist so universally that we must consider them also to be parts of normal personality.

Without necessarily subscribing to any of the numerous theories of personality, it is possible to describe personality in terms of certain important aspects or elements. We are all aware of ourselves as thinking organisms.

This aspect of personality, the conscious part, is important for understanding human behavior, but it is not enough. Many find it hard to accept the notion that each person also has an unconscious. The existence of the unconscious is no longer a matter of debate. It is not possible to estimate at all precisely what proportion of our total psychological life is conscious, what proportion unconscious. Everyone who has studied the problem, however, agrees that consciousness is the smaller part of personality. Most of what we are and do is a result of unconscious processes. To ignore this is to risk mistakes.

14. The above passage suggests that an interviewer can be MOST effective if he 14.____
    A. learns how to determine other peoples' unconscious motivations
    B. learns how to repress his own unconsciously motivated mannerisms and behavior
    C. can keep others from feeling that he either likes or dislikes them
    D. gains an understanding of how the unconscious operates in himself and in others

15. It may be inferred from the above passage that the *subtle processes*, such as gestures, posture, voice intonation, or choice of words referred to in the first paragraph are USUALLY 15.____
    A. in the complete control of an expert investigator
    B. the determining factors in the friendships a person establishes
    C. controlled by a person's unconscious
    D. not capable of being consciously controlled

16. The above passage implies that various different personality theories are USUALLY 16.____
    A. so numerous and different as to be valueless to an investigator
    B. in basic agreement about the importance of the unconscious
    C. understood by the investigator who strives to be effective
    D. in agreement that personality factors such as projection and repression are pathological

Questions 17-19.

DIRECTIONS: Questions 17 through 19 are to be answered SOLELY on the basis of information contained in the following passage.

No matter how well the interrogator adjusts himself to the witness and how precisely he induces the witness to describe his observations, mistakes still can be made. The mistakes made by an experienced interrogator may be comparatively few, but as far as the witness is concerned, his path is full of pitfalls. Modern "witness psychology" has shown that even the most honest and trustworthy witnesses are apt to make grave mistakes in good faith. It is, therefore, necessary that the interrogator get an idea of the weak links in the testimony in order to check up on them in the event that something appears to be strange or not quite satisfactory.

Unfortunately, modern witness psychology does not yet offer any means of directly testing the credibility of testimony. It lacks precision and method, in spite of worthwhile attempts on the part of learned men. At the same time, witness psychology, through the gathering of many experience concerning the weaknesses of human testimony, has been of invaluable service. It shows clearly that only evidence of a technical nature has absolute value as proof.

Testimony may be separated into the following stages: (1) perception; (2) observation; (3) mind fixation of the observed occurrences, in which fantasy, association of ideas, and personal judgment participate; (4) expression in oral or written form, where the testimony is transferred from one witness to another or to the interrogator. Each of these stages offers innumerable possibilities for the distortion of testimony.

17. The above passage indicates that having witnesses talk to each other before testifying is a practice which is GENERALLY 17.____
    A. *desirable*, since the witnesses will be able to correct each other's errors in observation before testimony
    B. *undesirable*, since the witnesses will collaborate on one story to tell the investigator
    C. *undesirable*, since one witness may distort his testimony because of what another witness may erroneously say
    D. *desirable*, since witnesses will become aware of discrepancies in their own testimony and can point out the discrepancies to the investigator

18. According to the above passage, the one of the following which would be the MOST reliable for use as evidence would be the testimony of a 18.____
    A. handwriting expert about a signature on a forged check
    B. trained police officer about the identity of a criminal
    C. laboratory technician about an accident he has observed
    D. psychologist who has interviewed any witness who relate conflicting stories

19. Concerning the validity of evidence, it is clear from the above passage that 19.____
    A. only evidence of a technical nature is at all valuable
    B. the testimony of witnesses is so flawed that it is usually valueless
    C. an investigator, by knowing modern witness psychology, will usually be able to perceive mistaken testimony
    D. an investigator ought to expect mistakes in even the most reliable witness testimony

Questions 20-21.

DIRECTIONS: Questions 20 and 21 are to be answered SOLELY on the basis of information given in the following passage.

Since we generally assure informants that what they say is confidential, we are not free to tell one informant what the other has told us. Even if the informant says, "*I don't care who knows it; tell anybody you want to,*" we find it wise to treat the interview as confidential. An interviewer who relates to some informants what other informants have told him is likely to stir up anxiety and suspicion. Of course, the interviewer may be able to tell an informant what he has heard without revealing the source of his information. This may be perfectly appropriate where a story has wide currency so that an informant cannot infer the source of the information. But if an event is not widely known, the mere mention of it may reveal to one informant what another informant has said about the situation. How can the data be cross-checked in these circumstances.

20. The above passage IMPLIES that the anxiety and suspicion an interviewer may arouse by telling what has been learned in other interviews is due to the 20._____
    A. lack of trust the person interviewed may have in the interviewer's honesty
    B. troublesome nature of the material which the interviewer has learned in other interviews
    C. fact that the person interviewed may not believe that permission was given to repeat the information
    D. fear of the person interviewed that what he is telling the interviewer will be repeated

21. The above passage is MOST likely part of a longer passage dealing with 21._____
    A. ways to verify data gathered in interviews
    B. the various anxieties a person being interviewed may feel
    C. the notion that people sometimes say things they do not mean
    D. ways an interview can avoid seeming suspicious

Questions 22-23.

DIRECTIONS: Questions 22 and 23 are to be answered SOLELY on the basis of information given below.

The ability to interview rests not on any single trait, but on a vast complex of them. Habits, skills, techniques, and attitudes are all involved. Competence in interviewing is acquired only after careful and diligent study, prolonged practice (preferably under supervision), and a good bit of trial and error; for interviewing is not an exact science; it is an art. Like many other arts, however, it can and must draw on science in several of its aspects.

There is always a place for individual initiative, for imaginative innovations, and for new combinations of old approaches. The skilled interviewer cannot be bound by a set of rules. Likewise, there is not a set of rules which can guarantee to the novice that his interviewing will be successful. There are, however, some accepted, general guideposts which may help the beginner to avoid mistakes, learn how to conserve this efforts, and establish effective working relationships with interviewees; to accomplish, in short, what he sets out to do.

22. According to the above passage, rules and standard techniques for interviewing are 22.____
    A. helpful for the beginner, but useless for the experienced, innovative interviewer
    B. destructive of the innovation and initiative needed for a good interviewer
    C. useful for even the experienced interviewer who may, however, sometimes go beyond them
    D. the means by which nearly anybody can become an effective interviewer

23. According to the above passage, the one of the following which is a prerequisite to competent interviewing is 23.____
    A. avoid mistakes
    B. study and practice
    C. imaginative innovation
    D. natural aptitude

Questions 24-27.

DIRECTIONS: Questions 24 through 27 are to be answered SOLELY on the basis of information given in the following passage.

The question of what material is relevant is not as simple as it might seem. Frequently, material which seems irrelevant to the inexperienced has, because of the common tendency to disguise and distort and misplace one's feelings, considerable significance. It may be necessary to let the client "ramble on" for a while in order to clear the decks, as it were, so that he may get down to things that really are on his mind. On the other hand, with an already disturbed person, it may be important for the interviewer to know when to discourage further elaboration of upsetting material. This is especially the case where the worker would be unable to do anything about it. An inexperienced interviewer might, for instance, be intrigued with the bizarre elaboration of material that the psychotic produces, but further elaboration of this might encourage the client in his instability. A too random discussion may indicate that the interviewee is not certain in what areas the interviewer is prepared to help him, and he may be seeking some direction. Or again, satisfying though it may be for the interviewer to have the interviewee tell him intimate details, such revelations sometimes need to be checked or encouraged only in small doses. An interviewee who has "talked too much" often reveals subsequent anxiety. This is illustrated by the fact that frequently after a "confessional" interview, the interviewee surprises the interviewer by being withdrawn, inarticulate, or hostile, or by breaking the next appointment.

24. Sometimes a client may reveal certain personal information to an interviewer and subsequently may feel anxious about this revelation. 24.____
    If, during an interview, a client begins to discuss very personal matters, it would be BEST to
    A. tell the client, in no uncertain terms, that you're not interested in personal details
    B. ignore the client at this point
    C. encourage the client to elaborate further on the details
    D. inform the client that the information seems to be very personal

25. The author indicates that clients with severe psychological disturbances pose an especially difficult problem for the inexperienced interviewer. 25.____
The difficulty lies in the possibility of the client
    A. becoming physically violent and harming the interviewer
    B. rambling on for a while
    C. revealing irrelevant details which may be followed by cancelled appointments
    D. reverting to an unstable state as a result of interview material

26. An interviewer should be constantly alert to the possibility of obtaining clues from the client as to the problem areas. 26.____
According to the above passage, a client who discusses topics at random may be
    A. unsure of what problems the interviewer can provide help with
    B. reluctant to discuss intimate details
    C. trying to impress the interviewer with his knowledge
    D. deciding what relevant material to elaborate on

27. The evaluation of a client's responses may reveal substantial information that may aid the interviewer in assessing the problem areas that are of concern to the client. Responses that seemed irrelevant at the time of the interview may be of significance because 27.____
    A. considerable significance is attached to all relevant material
    B. emotional feelings are frequently masked
    C. an initial *rambling on* is often a prelude to what is actually bothering the client
    D. disturbed clients often reveal subsequent anxiety

Questions 28-30.

DIRECTIONS: Questions 28 through 30 are to be answered SOLELY on the basis of the following passage.

The physical setting of the interview may determine its entire potentiality. Some degree of privacy and a comfortable relaxed atmosphere are important. The interviewee is not encouraged to give much more than his name and address if the interviewer seems busy with other things, if people are rushing about, if there are distracting noises. He has a right to feel that, whether the interview lasts five minutes or an hour, he has, for that time, the undivided attention of the interviewer. Interruptions, telephone calls, and so on, should be reduced to a minimum. If the interviewee has waited in a crowded room for what seems to him an interminably long period, he is naturally in mood to sit down and discuss what is on his mind. Indeed, by that time, the primary thing on his mind may be his irritation at being kept waiting, and he frequently feels it would be impolite to express this. If a wait or interruptions have been unavoidable, it is always helpful to give the client some recognition that these are disturbing and that we can naturally understand that they make it more difficult for him to proceed. At the same time, if he protests that they have not troubled him, the interviewer can best accept his statements at their face value, as further insistence that they must have been disturbing may be interpreted by him as accusing, and he may conclude that the interviewer has been personally hurt by his irritation.

28. Distraction during an interview may tend to limit the client's responses. In a case where an interruption has occurred, it would be BEST for the investigator to 28.____
   A. terminate this interview and have it rescheduled for another time period
   B. ignore the interruption since it is not continuous
   C. express his understanding that the distraction can cause the client to feel disturbed
   D. accept the client's protests that he has been troubled by the interruption

29. To maximize the rapport that can be established with the client, an appropriate physical setting is necessary. At the very least, some privacy would be necessary. In addition, the interviewer should 29.____
   A. always appear to be busy in order to impress the client
   B. focus his attention only on the client
   C. accept all the client's statements as being valid
   D. stress the importance of the interview to the client

30. Clients who have been waiting quite some time for their interview may, justifiably, become upset. However, a client may initially attempt to mask these feelings because he may 30.____
   A. personally hurt the interviewer
   B. want to be civil
   C. feel that the wait was unavoidable
   D. fear the consequences of his statement

KEY (CORRECT ANSWERS)

1.	B	11.	A	21.	A
2.	C	12.	B	22.	C
3.	D	13.	D	23.	B
4.	D	14.	D	24.	D
5.	B	15.	C	25.	D
6.	D	16.	B	26.	A
7.	C	17.	C	27.	B
8.	C	18.	A	28.	C
9.	D	19.	D	29.	B
10.	C	20.	D	30.	B

TEST 2

DIRECTIONS: Each question or incomplete statement is followed by several suggested answers or completions. Select the one that BEST answers the question or completes the statement. *PRINT THE LETTER OF THE CORRECT ANSWER IN THE SPACE AT THE RIGHT.*

Questions 1-5.

DIRECTIONS: In Questions 1 through 5, choose the statement which is BEST from the point of view of English usage suitable for a business report.

1. A. The client's receiving of public assistance checks at two different addresses were disclosed by the investigation. 1.____
   B. The investigation disclosed that the client was receiving public assistance checks at two different addresses.
   C. The client was found out by the investigator to be receiving public assistance checks at two different addresses.
   D. The client has been receiving public assistance checks at two different addresses, disclosed the investigation

2. A. The investigation of complaints are usually handled by this unit, which deals with internal security problems in the department. 2.____
   B. This unit deals with internal security problems in the department; usually investigating complaints.
   C. Investigating complaints is this unit's job, being that it handles internal security problems in the department
   D. This unit deals with internal security problems in the department and usually investigates complaints.

3. A. The delay in completing this investigation was caused by difficulty in obtaining the required documents from the candidate. 3.____
   B. Because of difficulty in obtaining the required documents from the candidate is the reason that there was a delay in completing this investigation.
   C. Having had difficulty in obtaining the required documents from the candidate, there was a delay in completing this investigation.
   D. Difficulty in obtaining the required documents from the candidate had the affect of delaying the completion of this investigation.

4. A. This report, together with documents supporting our recommendation, are being submitted for your approval. 4.____
   B. Documents supporting our recommendation is being submitted with the report for your approval.
   C. This report, together with documents supporting our documentation, is being submitted for your approval.
   D. The report and documents supporting our recommendation is being submitted for your approval.

5. A. Several people were interviewed and numerous letters were sent before this case was completed. 5.____
B. Completing this case, interviewing several people and sending numerous letters were necessary.
C. To complete this case needed interviewing several people and sending numerous letters.
D. Interviewing several people and sending numerous letters was necessary to complete the case.

Questions 6-20.

DIRECTIONS: For each of the sentences numbered 6 to 20, select from the options given below the MOST applicable choice, and mark your answer accordingly.
A. The sentence is correct.
B. The sentence contains a spelling error only.
C. The sentence contains an English grammar error only.
D. The sentence contains both a spelling error and an English grammar error.

6. He is a very dependible person whom we expect will be an asset to this division. 6.____

7. An investigator often finds it necessary to be very diplomatic when conducting an interview. 7.____

8. Accurate detail is especially important if court action results from an investigation. 8.____

9. The report was signed by him and I since we conducted the investigation jointly. 9.____

10. Upon receipt of the complaint, an inquiry was begun. 10.____

11. An employee has to organize his time so that he can handle his workload efficiantly. 11.____

12. It was not apparent that anyone was living at the address given by the client. 12.____

13. According to regulations, there is to be at least three attempts made to locate the client. 13.____

14. Neither the inmate nor the correction officer was willing to sign a formal statement. 14.____

15. It is our opinion that one of the persons interviewed were lying. 15.____

16. We interviewed both clients and departmental personel in the course of this investigation. 16.____

17. It is concievable that further research might produce additional evidence. 17.____

18. There are too many occurences of this nature to ignore. 18.____

19. We cannot accede to the candidate's request. 19.____

20. The submission of overdue reports is the reason that there was a delay in completion of this investigation. 20.____

Questions 21-2.

DIRECTIONS: Each of Questions 21 through 25 consists of three sentences lettered A, B, and C. In each of these questions, one of the sentences may contain an error in grammar, sentence structure, or punctuation, or all three sentences may be correct. If one of the sentences in a question contains an error in grammar, sentence structure, or punctuation, print in the space at the right the capital letter preceding the sentence which contains the error. If all three sentences are correct, print the letter D.

21. A. Mr. Smith appears to be less competent than I in performing these duties. 21.____
B. The supervisor spoke to the employee, who had made the error, but did not reprimand him.
C. When he found the book lying on the table, he immediately notified the owner.

22. A. Being locked in the desk, we were certain that the papers would not be taken. 22.____
B. It wasn't I who dictated the telegram; I believe it was Eleanor.
C. You should interview whoever comes to the office today.

23. A. The clerk was instructed to set the machine on the table before summoning the manager. 23.____
B. He said that he was not familiar with those kind of activities.
C. A box of pencils, in addition to erasers and blotters, was included in the shipment.

24. A. The supervisor remarked, "Assigning an employee to the proper type of work is not always easy." 24.____
B. The employer found that each of the applicants were qualified to perform the duties of the position.
C. Any competent student is permitted to take this course if he obtains the consent of the instructor.

25. A. The prize was awarded to the employee whom the judges believed to be most deserving. 25.____
B. Since the instructor believes this book is the better of the two, he is recommending it for use in the school.
C. It was obvious to the employees that the completion of the task by the scheduled date would require their working overtime.

KEY (CORRECT ANSWERS)

1. B
2. D
3. A
4. C
5. A

6. D
7. A
8. A
9. C
10. A

11. B
12. B
13. C
14. A
15. C

16. B
17. B
18. B
19. A
20. C

21. B
22. A
23. B
24. B
25. D

EFFECTIVELY INTERACTING WITH AGENCY STAFF AND MEMBERS OF THE PUBLIC

Test material will be presented in a multiple-choice question format.

Test Task: You will be presented with a variety of situations in which you must apply knowledge of how best to interact with other people.

SAMPLE QUESTION:

A person approaches you expressing anger about a recent action by your department. Which one of the following should be your first response to this person?

A. Interrupt to say you cannot discuss the situation until he calms down.
B. Say you are sorry that he has been negatively affected by your department's action.
C. Listen and express understanding that he has been upset by your department's action.
D. Give him an explanation of the reasons for your department's action.

The CORRECT answer to this sample question is Choice C.
Solution:

Choice A is not correct. It would be inappropriate to interrupt. In addition, saying that you cannot discuss the situation until the person calms down will likely aggravate the person further.

Choice B is not correct. Apologizing for your department's action implies that the action was improper.

Choice C is the correct answer to this question. By listening and expressing understanding that your department's action has upset the person, you demonstrate that you have heard and understand the person's feelings and point of view.

Choice D is not correct. While an explanation of the reasons for the action may be appropriate at a later time, at this moment the person is angry and would not be receptive to such an explanation.

EXAMINATION SECTION

TEST 1

DIRECTIONS: Each question or incomplete statement is followed by several suggested answers or completions. Select the one that BEST answers the question or completes the statement. *PRINT THE LETTER OF THE CORRECT ANSWER IN THE SPACE AT THE RIGHT.*

1. Which of the following are covered under the definition of customer service? 1.____
   A. A positive environment set up to efficiently handle customer requests
   B. Infrastructure designed to distribute merchandise in a timely fashion
   C. Employees filling distinct roles to meet customer needs
   D. All of the above

2. An organization that has a clearly established customer service approach can distinguish itself from competitors. This is referred to as the organization's 2.____
   A. customer prioritization
   B. service culture
   C. imagineering
   D. none of the above

3. The physical space of a hospitality setting is MOST commonly referred to as the 3.____
   A. customer landscape
   B. business policy
   C. servicescape
   D. arena of service

4. When dealing with a customer, one must be knowledgeable, capable and enthusiastic when delivering products and/or services and it must be done in a manner that satisfies 4.____
   A. both identified and unidentified needs
   B. local and global competition
   C. quality and quantity of goods/services
   D. all demands of the customer

5. Employees at the center learn at their orientation that services are inseparable because service quality and customer satisfaction are largely dependent on which of the following? 5.____
   A. Interactions between employees and customers
   B. Uniform offerings for individuals
   C. Establishing patents for individual services
   D. All of the above

6. An organization with a strong customer service culture 6.____
   A. allows employees to use their own initiative to solve customer problems
   B. has policies that allow employees to easily please customers
   C. provides extensive customer service training for employees
   D. all of the above

7. Which of the following is TRUE of customer contact through electronic mail? 7.____
   A. Be sure to use all caps for important aspects of the e-mail
   B. State the purpose of the message clearly
   C. Do not feel the need to respond immediately
   D. Include lengthy descriptions in the body of the e-mail

8. A clerk is speaking to residents at a zoning committee meeting and uses the word “coulda” instead of “could have” in his presentation. 8.____
This is an example of
   A. good enunciation
   B. poor tone
   C. poor enunciation
   D. proper pitch

9. An employee is delivering a presentation to parents about the benefits of children joining summer camps when someone complains that the employee’s changing pitch makes it hard to hear what he is saying and that he needs to fix it. 9.____
What does the parent mean by fixing his pitch?
The employee needs to
   A. keep his voice from going too high or too low
   B. keep his voice from getting too soft or too loud
   C. keep his attitude towards certain subjects in check
   D. make sure his words are clearly spoken and not garbled

10. A clerk recently moved from answering phone calls every day to working face-to-face with residents. 10.____
Which of the following will help her be most successful when transferring from phone to personal communication?
   A. Focus on sharing only positive information
   B. Speak more authoritatively
   C. Maintain a more casual tone and familiarity with residents
   D. Positive communication through eye contact and body language

11. Talking via telephone 11.____
   A. is less personal than sending an e-mail message
   B. is a poor way to reach most residents
   C. can allow residents to receive instant feedback
   D. is not popular within public services

12. An employee is in charge of calling local homeowners to tell them about upcoming activities, and more often than not she needs to leave a voicemail. 12.____
Which of the following is the MOST effective way to leave voicemails?
   A. Be courteous
   B. Provide the appropriate information
   C. Contain lengthy details
   D. Both A and B

13. You are dealing with a parent who is upset about a miscommunication related to her child's application for an activity. Which of the following would be LEAST frustrating for the parent to hear from you? 13.____
   A. "I don't know. I will do my best."
   B. "Let me see what I can do for you."
   C. "I apologize, but you will have to..."
   D. "Oh, my manager should be able to help you, but he's not in right now."

14. If a part-time assistant employee should need to apologize to customers, which of the following should he NOT do when apologizing? 14.____
   A. Apologize right away
   B. Be sincere in his apology
   C. Make the apology personal
   D. Offer an official apology from the department

15. If a clerk's office is looking to improve its processes to increase community satisfaction, feedback received should be each of the following EXCEPT 15.____
   A. centered on internal customers
   B. ongoing
   C. available internally to everyone from employees to supervisors
   D. focused on a limited number of indicators

16. A member of the community has identified a flaw in one of the policies regarding town hall meetings. Now that the problem has been identified, all of the following should be steps toward resolving the issue EXCEPT 16.____
   A. following up on the problem resolution
   B. making whatever promises are necessary
   C. listening and responding to all complaints
   D. providing the resident with whatever was originally requested

17. When looking to achieve the best results as someone who interacts with the public, one should always strive to represent 17.____
   A. the entire organization B. the customer
   C. the department D. their direct supervisor

18. Approximately how long does it take a person on hold to become annoyed? 18.____
   A. 1 minute B. 40 seconds C. 20 seconds D. 2 minutes

19. If an employee answers the phone and is asked to transfer the call to a co-worker, which of the following would be the MOST appropriate response? 19.____
   A. "She isn't in right now, so I'll have to take a message."
   B. "She's still at lunch. Can I take a message?"
   C. "She should be back soon. Could you call back in 15 minutes?"
   D. "Let me transfer you. If she's not in, please leave a message and she will return your call."

20. A public employee has been specifically assigned to deal with public complaints because he is remarkably skilled at dealing with residents. Which of the following mentalities would explain why the employee is so effective at dealing with residents? 20.____
    A. They always cave in to whatever demands the residents make
    B. They effectively manage residents' expectations
    C. They always sincerely apologize no matter who is at fault
    D. Both A and C

21. When dealing with a frustrated customer, which of the following practices should an employee avoid? 21.____
    A. Immediately offer a solution to their problem
    B. Soothe the customer's frustration first
    C. Remain positive and non-confrontational with the customer
    D. Let the customer vent and feel like they've shared their feelings accurately

22. The town clerk's office in Avondale is highly rated by town residents. When surveyed, residents of Avondale claim that their town clerks always have such great customer service. Of the customer service techniques listed below, which one is MOST likely the reason for such high ratings? 22.____
    A. When dealing with abusive residents, Avondale clerks always hang up on them
    B. Clerks in Avondale have a readied list of solutions to resident problems, so they are able to offer personalized solutions right away
    C. Avondale clerks always follow up with residents who call or come in
    D. Clerks always look customers in the eye even when they are frustrated and upset

23. If a parent was told there would be space in a day camp for all of her children, and only two of them ended up being placed together, which of the following actions would be PROPER for a parks employee to take? 23.____
    A. Offer a sincere apology and attempt to fix the problem
    B. Promise the parent that all her children will be together even if it means dropping other children from the camp
    C. Explain the Parks Department policy regarding camp sign-up and tell the parent to contact a manager for further explanation
    D. Tell the parent she needs to speak to someone with more authority

24. If a person has a hearing impairment, which of the following practical solutions could a clerk have in place to help them? 24.____
    A. Reading a description of policy to the person
    B. Write a note to answer a question they have
    C. Read the words communicated by the person's "communication board"
    D. Assist the person in maneuvering through the physical space of the office

25. When dealing with a call, who should end the phone call first? 25.____
    A. The person who answered
    B. The person who called
    C. Either one – it doesn't matter
    D. A manager

KEY (CORRECT ANSWERS)

1.	D	11.	C
2.	B	12.	D
3.	C	13.	B
4.	A	14.	D
5.	A	15.	A
6.	D	16.	B
7.	B	17.	A
8.	C	18.	C
9.	A	19.	D
10.	D	20.	B

21.	A
22.	C
23.	A
24.	B
25.	B

TEST 2

DIRECTIONS: Each question or incomplete statement is followed by several suggested answers or completions. Select the one that BEST answers the question or completes the statement. *PRINT THE LETTER OF THE CORRECT ANSWER IN THE SPACE AT THE RIGHT.*

1. Which of the following would be considered acceptable for an office clerk when answering the phone? 1.____
   A. Chewing gum
   B. Listening to music
   C. Eating a snack while on mute
   D. Wearing a headset

2. Why would asking a caller for their phone number be important? 2.____
   A. In case they get disconnected
   B. To show them you are polite and considerate
   C. In case the caller is rude, this way you can call them back
   D. For future instances where calling residents back might make sense

3. When rolling out a new program to help train employees in better customer service, the manager starts off by talking about the importance of telephone greetings. 3.____
   Why is this so important?
   A. It is the first impression the customer has of the department
   B. It shows the customer that employees are happy
   C. It shows that you are polite
   D. It isn't that important, but the manager thinks it is

4. Which of the following is the MOST important aspect of an employee's voice in a telephone call? 4.____
   A. Their volume
   B. Their speed
   C. Their tone
   D. All of these aspects are equally important

5. A clerk is on the phone with a customer when another customer walks into the building. 5.____
   If the clerk must put the caller on hold, what do they need to say or ask?
   A. "Would you like to be put on hold?"
   B. "I apologize for the inconvenience, but please hold."
   C. "Would it be OK if I put you on hold for a moment?"
   D. "I have to let you go. Please call back later."

6. When a resident comes into your office for a face-to-face meeting, it is of increased importance that you communicate positively with your 6.____
   A. words
   B. body language
   C. tone
   D. none of the above

7. A customer calls when employees are at an all-staff meeting. When calling the customer back, a clerk reaches their voicemail. 7.____
Which of the following information is the MOST important to leave?
   A. The date and time
   B. Ask them to call back
   C. The employee's telephone number
   D. Apologize repeatedly for missing their call

8. If an employee is in the middle of a conversation about town hall policy with a co-worker and the phone rings, what should the employee do? 8.____
   A. Get caller's information and call back after the conversation is finished
   B. Tell the co-worker to wait until finished with the phone call
   C. Answer the call and put caller on hold until conversation is finished
   D. Answer the call and transfer it to another employee who is not currently busy

9. When dealing with a resident who casually uses vulgar language, it is MOST appropriate for a town employee to 9.____
   A. tell the resident to come back when he learns how to speak
   B. converse with the resident using equally coarse language
   C. politely ask the resident to refrain from using vulgar language
   D. make the resident wait longer so he knows it won't be tolerated

10. The mayor's office has recently come under fire for a variety of perceived scandals. 10.____
In this emergency situation, which of the following would NOT be a recommended step in handling the crisis?
   A. Minimizing damage to the office's reputation through whatever means necessary
   B. Taking responsibility and apologizing
   C. Providing constant updates on the situation
   D. Designating one spokesperson to handle the relaying of updates

11. A resident complains that recreation center employees are using bureaucratic or overly technical communication. This type of language is often referred to as 11.____
   A. clichés B. jargon C. euphemisms D. legalese

12. Which of the following strategies does an employee need to utilize to convince the public to believe a message that is contrary to their beliefs? 12.____
   A. Cognitive dissonance
   B. Uses and gratification
   C. Sleeper effect
   D. Source credibility

13. When communicating with parents of a summer camp run by the district, which of the following should NOT be a goal of the process? 13.____
   A. Motivation
   B. Persuasion
   C. Mutual understanding
   D. Isolation of the conflict

14. A manager comes up with a new procedure that he believes would improve the claims process that residents need to go through. Some employees agree that the procedure would make sense and others do not. One employee openly criticizes the idea to the manager. 14.____
Which of the following actions should the manager take?
He should
   A. meet with the employee for a talk and explain why bypassing his authority is unacceptable
   B. not respond to the critics in order to avoid unnecessary risks
   C. reprimand the employee who went over his head
   D. only implement the procedures that all agreed were good in order to satisfy employees

15. The county clerk's office is working on improving its employees' professionalism. 15.____
If employees are attempting to maintain a professional demeanor, what should they NOT do after making a mistake?
   A. Work to do better at the next opportunity
   B. Move on
   C. Accept responsibility
   D. Explain or rationalize the error

16. According to most recent surveys, data reveals that most white-collar workers 16.____
   A. have about a 25 percent efficiency rate when listening
   B. lose only about 25 percent efficiency when listening
   C. never take listening for granted
   D. learn to listen effectively since hearing is the important active learned process

17. Which of the following are NOT one of the four phases of listening to a customer? 17.____
   A. Hearing B. Translating C. Responding D. Comprehending

18. Which of the following societal factors might impact a resident/employee interaction? 18.____
   A. Increased efficiency in technology
   B. Globalization of the economy
   C. More people between the ages of 16-24 entering the workplace
   D. Geopolitical changes

19. If a resident comes in confused about a policy change, which of the following approaches should an employee take to handle the situation? 19.____
   A. Communicate negatively when they need to
   B. Avoid gestures such as smiling or looking at customers when speaking to them
   C. Recognize how they tend to communicate and adjust accordingly if the customer is still showing signs of confusion
   D. Understand that many people are doubtful of good customer service

20. In order to avoid negative public perception, which of the following "finger pointing" words/phrases should be avoided when interacting with the public? 20.____
    A. Let me B. You C. Why D. Yes

21. In an effort to improve government/resident relations, the mayor wants to roll out a new PR format that stresses public communication. 21.____
    Which of the following strategies should NOT be suggested as part of the PR campaign?
    A. Plan the message
    B. Greet residents warmly
    C. Listen carefully and respond appropriately
    D. Let the residents initiate conversations

22. A resident complains that the department does not always treat the local residents as people. 22.____
    Of the following, which would be the BEST strategy for resolving this issue?
    A. Accept responsibility and offer specific assistance
    B. Blame the customer when necessary
    C. Provide policies as reasons for actions
    D. None of the above

23. When providing feedback to residents, which of the following strategies is NOT effective? 23.____
    A. Remain emotional when providing feedback
    B. Confirm residents' meaning before offering feedback
    C. Ensure the feedback is appropriate to the original message
    D. Avoid extreme criticism or negative language

24. An employee at City Hall receives special treatment from his manager. This causes the employee to feel empowered, which then leads to him abusing authority and power. 24.____
    Which of the following would MOST likely happen if this behavior is allowed to continue?
    A. Other employees would begin to feel empowered
    B. Co-workers would work harder to demonstrate their commitment
    C. Residents would begin to work with the empowered employee because he would be able to get things done
    D. The rest of the department would start to feel resentment and frustration, and might potentially retaliate

25. If a town clerk works well with customers on the phone but struggles with face-to-face interactions, which of the following might BEST explain the problem? 25.____
    A. The actual words the clerk uses B. Facial and other body cues
    C. Vocal cues D. Both A and C

KEY (CORRECT ANSWERS)

1. D
2. A
3. A
4. D
5. C

6. B
7. C
8. B
9. C
10. A

11. B
12. A
13. D
14. A
15. D

16. A
17. B
18. C
19. C
20. B

21. D
22. A
23. A
24. D
25. B

TEST 3

DIRECTIONS: Each question or incomplete statement is followed by several suggested answers or completions. Select the one that BEST answers the question or completes the statement. *PRINT THE LETTER OF THE CORRECT ANSWER IN THE SPACE AT THE RIGHT.*

1. If an employee's body position is causing customers to feel she is projecting a mood/attitude that she isn't actually expressing, what does the employee need to work on improving? 1.____
   A. Pitch B. Articulation C. Posture D. Inflection

2. A newly hired assistant notices that everyone in his department has received a new computer system except for him. 2.____
   What should he do?
   A. Assume this is a mistake and speak to his manager
   B. Complain to H.R.
   C. Quit
   D. Confront his manager regarding his unfair treatment

3. A team leader in your department notices that ample amounts of department-labeled property have come up missing in recent weeks. The leader notices a fellow supervisor putting stationery and other equipment into a personal bag on a few different occasions and believes this person is responsible. 3.____
   What is the LEAST effective response to the situation?
   A. Gather more evidence to catch the person in the act
   B. Do nothing – if guilty, someone else will likely catch the colleague
   C. Privately ask other colleagues if they've noticed anything suspicious recently
   D. Inform a supervisor higher up in the organization that this person is a potential suspect

4. Near the end of the work day, an official advisor accidentally sends an e-mail containing confidential information to the wrong person. 4.____
   Which of the following would be the BEST thing for the advisor to do?
   A. Overlook the error. Send the e-mail to the correct person and leave things as they are.
   B. Find a senior advisor and explain the mistake and have them deal with the problem
   C. Leave the office and deal with any fallout tomorrow
   D. Immediately send a follow-up e-mail to the "wrong" person explaining the mistake. Then send the e-mail to the correct person.

5. If an employee is engaged with a customer and no one else is around when the phone rings, what is the PROPER step to take in this situation? 5.____
   A. Let the phone ring and continue to work with the customer in person
   B. Take the call and address the caller's issue, then hang up and come back to the customer
   C. Ask the customer to answer the phone while trying to resolve their issue.
   D. Tell the customer "excuse me" while answering the phone, then put the caller on hold while going back to the customer

6. According to many national retailer surveys, what do consumers remember the MOST about their customer service experience? 6.____
   A. The cost of the merchandise/experience
   B. The demeanor of the employee who engaged them
   C. The cleanliness of the office/area
   D. How nice the employees were

7. When attempting to help a resident make a decision about programs offered by your agency, it is important to remember that the majority of purchasing decisions consumers make are based upon 7.____
   A. what they think
   B. a potential free gift
   C. how they feel
   D. all of the above

8. In an effort to improve procedures in your department, a memo has been sent to employees. In it, one highlighted section focuses on the importance of avoiding closed-ended questions/comments. 8.____
   Following the advice of the memo, which question/comment should an employee avoid stating to a resident?
   A. "Can I help you?"
   B. "What is it you would like to see accomplished?"
   C. "So the challenges you've faced so far are…"
   D. "How would you like to see that improved?"

9. Numerous surveys indicate that consumers would actually pay more for 9.____
   A. self-checkout machines
   B. free product/demonstration giveaways
   C. more streamlined customer service
   D. apps using customer-service bots

10. Which of the following is an example of a proper "Activation Greeting"? 10.____
   A. "My name is _____. Let me tell you about our programs."
   B. "How many are there in your group?"
   C. "Hi! Welcome to _____."
   D. Both A and C

11. When interacting with members of the public, which of the following is the MOST important thing to do? 11.____
    A. Ask them to pay for services up front
    B. Smile at them
    C. Learn their name and call them by it
    D. Ask questions

12. Which of the following pieces of advice would help a clerk the MOST when working with the public? 12.____
    A. Pay attention to needs of others and offer only general solutions
    B. Hear what others are saying but do not take their comments to heart
    C. Focus on efficiency of service over quality of service
    D. Clearly understand the motives and needs of others

13. A member of the community complains that counselors at her child's camp do not listen to what she is telling them. 13.____
    Which technique listed below would improve understanding between the two parties?
    A. Reflective listening
    B. Narrow selections
    C. Reflective thinking
    D. Valid suggestions

14. When dealing with elderly residents, which of the following facts should be considered by a public official? 14.____
    A. They expect to be treated with courtesy and respect
    B. Expect them to avoid eye contact
    C. They prefer the telephone to personal contact
    D. They expect text and e-mail over face-to-face communication

15. If you are hired as a camp counselor for younger residents, it is important to remember all of the following about their behavior EXCEPT that they 15.____
    A. value technology
    B. are used to multitasking and access to instant information
    C. make less eye contact
    D. prefer more formal interactions

16. If one is trying to improve morale regarding customer/worker relations, which of the following is NOT a recommended thing to do? 16.____
    A. Publicly embarrass customers who are rude to the office employees
    B. Greet the customer with "Good Morning"
    C. Politely ask customers who cut in line to wait until it is their turn
    D. Thank customers for doing business with you

17. When hired by a public office, which of the following would be part of the newly hired employee's performance code? 17.____
    A. Report on time in a calm and controlled manner
    B. Present oneself in a neat and clean way
    C. Treat co-workers and residents with dignity and respect
    D. All of the above

18. If an employee sometimes "bends the rules" to honor a request from a customer, what service concept would explain this action? 18.____
    A. Motivated marketing strategy
    B. Power selling philosophy
    C. Employee empowerment
    D. Selling out for the customer

19. A Parks and Recreation worker is attempting to improve relations with the groups who sign up for his arts and crafts program. 19.____
    He should remember all of the following "Customer Service Rules" EXCEPT
    A. Customer service has a large effect on customer satisfaction
    B. Modern consumers are already more satisfied with customer service today than ever before
    C. Modern consumers have many different mechanisms by which to complain
    D. Feeling empowered as an employee usually leads to higher customer satisfaction

20. A marketing executive employee wishes to emphasize customer loyalty. 20.____
    Which of the following marketing strategies should the employee focus on when working with customers?
    A. Relationship marketing
    B. Undercover marketing
    C. Diversity marketing
    D. Transactional marketing

21. Why would a campaign manager for an elected official be interested in conducting a mail survey over other methods of surveying? 21.____
    It would
    A. avoid non-response problems
    B. speed up the process by which surveys are returned to them
    C. avoid participation by incorrect respondents
    D. enable the completion of the survey at a convenient time

22. At the end of each session, a counselor takes it upon herself to conduct research on the effectiveness of the program. She is worried that respondents won't be truthful, so she decides that the BEST way to avoid bias would be to conduct a(n) _____ survey. 22.____
    A. personal
    B. telephone
    C. internet
    D. observational

23. A resident walks into the office and submits an application. When she is given additional forms to complete, she grumbles about "bureaucratic red tape" and how it's slowing down her application approval. 23.____
    How should an employee handle this situation?
    A. Be patient with the resident but do not explain the reason for the forms
    B. Tell the resident why the additional forms are necessary
    C. Suggest that the resident take it up with the manager if she wants the policy changed
    D. Say that the application will not be processed until ALL forms are completed

24. An employee's next-door neighbor has been hired as summer help, which the employee knows about because he has to type a confidential letter from the director to human resources about the hire. The neighbor does not yet know of the hiring decision, and the employee will see the neighbor later that day. Which one of the following should the employee do? 24.____
    A. Say nothing and wait for the offer to become official
    B. Congratulate the neighbor confidentially
    C. Inform a handful of people including the neighbor's close friends
    D. None of the above

25. A child with vision impairment wants to join a summer day camp and is denied access because the camp focuses on games and activities in which sight is required. If the parent comes in and complains to you, which of the following actions should you take and why? 25.____
    A. Modify the camp so the child can join because it is bad publicity to deny a child with a disability
    B. Offer another camp that does not focus on so many "sight-based" activities at a reduced rate so the parent and child do not feel left out
    C. Enroll the child and ensure they are allowed to participate in a meaningful way, because it's against the law to prevent the child from signing up
    D. Tell the parent they can talk to a supervisor because you have no authority to change the decision

---

KEY (CORRECT ANSWERS)

1.	C	11.	B
2.	A	12.	D
3.	B	13.	A
4.	D	14.	A
5.	D	15.	D
6.	B	16.	A
7.	C	17.	D
8.	A	18.	C
9.	C	19.	B
10.	C	20.	A

21.	D
22.	C
23.	B
24.	A
25.	C

TEST 4

DIRECTIONS: Each question or incomplete statement is followed by several suggested answers or completions. Select the one that BEST answers the question or completes the statement. *PRINT THE LETTER OF THE CORRECT ANSWER IN THE SPACE AT THE RIGHT.*

1. If a customer tells an employee they need to work on having open body language, which of the following would be an example? 1.____
   A. Fiddling
   B. Minimal eye contact
   C. Folded arms
   D. Frequent hand gestures

2. As a phone operator for the bureau director's office, it is important that you make the constituents feel as though you are actively listening to their concerns. What is the MOST effective way to demonstrate this? 2.____
   A. Use affirmation with words like "ok", "yes" and "I understand"
   B. Interrupt with your own thoughts
   C. Ask numerous closed questions
   D. Talk over the constituent

3. When a resident walks up to a clerk's desk, which of the following is the BEST way to greet them? 3.____
   A. Wave
   B. Ask them what they need
   C. Welcome them and ask how they can be helped
   D. Ignore them until finished with the current task

4. When a customer complains through e-mail, an office clerk should 4.____
   A. forward the e-mail to a supervisor
   B. reply right away with a potential solution
   C. share the complaint via the office's official Twitter handle
   D. reply right away with a hurried answer

5. Interacting with the public is a constant back and forth where feedback is essential to improving service. Which of the following methods would be BEST to obtain feedback from the public? 5.____
   A. Cold calling
   B. Tweeting
   C. Survey via website
   D. Ask the staff what they think

6. If residents continually complain that clerks do not truly understand what they are trying to tell them, which of the following practices might help improve this communication barrier? 6.____
   A. Paraphrasing
   B. Encoding
   C. Rapport building
   D. Decoding

7. A customer complains to an employee and demands to see a supervisor. The employee is not sure to who to direct this angry customer. 7.____
Which of the following methods of illustrating hierarchy of the company would help the employee out?
A. Diagramming
B. Negotiation
C. Brainstorming
D. Organizational charts

8. A village clerk and a resident have a strong disagreement about how an office policy applies to their situation. A co-worker is asked to weigh in on the situation. 8.____
How should the co-worker handle the situation?
A. Take the employee's side since they have to work side by side
B. Try to help both parties walk away feeling like they got what they wanted
C. Take the resident's side since the office cannot afford bad publicity
D. Have a supervisor intervene – it's better to pass responsibility onto someone in power

9. A parent accuses your department of making generalizations about their child based on the group to which they belong. 9.____
Which of the following unfair, but common, ideas is the department being accused of?
A. Racism
B. Stereotyping
C. Confirmation bias
D. Rationale judgment

10. When a resident calls a government office, they expect the phone to be picked up by the _____ ring otherwise they feel as though their call is unimportant. 10.____
A. 1st
B. 4th
C. 3rd
D. 7th

11. When working directly with a consumer on the phone or in person, which of the following would be considered inappropriate? 11.____
A. Eating, drinking or chewing gum
B. Speaking slowly and enunciating clearly
C. Asking permission to put someone on hold
D. Wearing a headset

12. Someone calls village hall and is extremely upset by a policy change enacted in the last board meeting. They demand an explanation that the clerk does not have. 12.____
As the clerk tries to find the answer, how often should she update the angry caller on the status of the complaint (even if the clerk has no answer)?
A. 2-3 minutes
B. 35 seconds
C. 1 minute
D. Do not update them until an answer has been found

13. A resident is irate over how a co-worker of yours handled his claim process and now you have to handle his appeal. Throughout the process of filling out the necessary paperwork, this resident continues to not only berate the co-worker, but also starts complaining about how slow you are. In this stressful situation, why is it important to stay calm and not let the resident get to you? 13.____
    A. They could be having a bad day and your anger may make the situation worse
    B. You need to show the resident you are willing to take the time necessary to resolve his or her problem
    C. They might be violent and could end up hurting you
    D. Both A and B

14. An employee is calling residents to thank them for volunteering for a food drive. As the employee moves through his list, he accidentally dials the wrong number, and a person on the other line answers. What should the employee do? 14.____
    A. Apologize to the person for calling the wrong number
    B. Thank the person anyway
    C. Hang up before the person says anything else
    D. Try to sign the person up for the next food drive

15. Which of the following questions tell the customer that the employee wants to ensure that every need has been met before the interaction is over? 15.____
    A. "You've said everything you need to say, right?"
    B. "Is there anything else I can help you with?"
    C. "How can I help you today?"
    D. "Would you like me to transfer you to someone else?"

16. An elderly resident calls your department, but was trying to reach the Health and Sanitation Department. What should you do? 16.____
    A. Be polite
    B. Hastily transfer the person to the correct department
    C. Try to determine who they need to speak to and transfer them to that person directly if possible
    D. Both A and C

17. Which of the following would NOT be considered an example of good customer service? 17.____
    A. A parent waits three minutes to pick up their child from an after-school activity
    B. A clearly defined resolution process is in place for residents who have disagreements with public officials
    C. There is no line at the DMV, and a person waits 10 minutes before being serviced
    D. The park's pools briefly close at noon and 4 p.m. so they can be skimmed and checked for debris

18. A resident is angry about a zoning issue that prevents him from adding on to his garage. 18.____
When dealing with this customer, which of the following should an employee NOT do?
A. Acknowledge their emotion
B. Ask questions
C. Avoid escalating the argument
D. Agree that the code is silly

19. A resident comes into the office where you work and complains that he was screened out of a job because of a vision impairment. He asks if this is legal and what he should do. 19.____
You tell him it is not against the Americans With Disabilities Act if the employer screens him because
A. clients prefer not to be served by the disabled
B. a business cannot make a reasonable accommodation to work tasks for a specific disability
C. co-workers dislike working with the disabled
D. none of the above; ADA prevents any kind of "screening out" of disabled persons

20. During holidays and special events, the school office can sometimes be short-staffed, which requires all employees to know the different roles within the office. Some parents do not like when certain staff members act as the receptionist and those staff members do not like being the receptionist. 20.____
Since both sides do not like the employees in that role, the employees should
A. learn the receptionist's job and fill in when needed, but tell the principal that they, and parents, would prefer that they work in a different area
B. tell the principal they don't want to work as a receptionist and ask to be excused from that role
C. learn the receptionist's job, but when asked to fill in ask someone else to do it
D. ask the principal to excuse then from the training, and explain that other employees who the parents like more could fill in for them

21. In an attempt to promote the recreation center in a positive light, which of the following advertising strategies would be MOST credible to town residents? 21.____
A. Employees telling people how great the recreation center environment is
B. Have local celebrities endorse the recreation center as the place to be
C. Use current satisfied customers by having them "spread the word" about the recreation center
D. Offer incredible discounts to the first 25 new customers to sign up

22. When a clerk is tasked with setting up a Town Hall meeting, all of the following are important EXCEPT 22.____
A. spreading the word
B. having an audience-selected moderator
C. setting and following a schedule
D. keeping things moving

23. A librarian works in the computer lab and a patron comes to her and says, "My flash drive is full. I need to save the document I just created. Where can I get a new flash drive?" 23.____
How should the librarian respond?
    A. Offer to help the patron e-mail the document to himself and then show him how to do it
    B. Ask the patron what he needs to save and then save it to a "Google Document" for them
    C. Offer him the use of a library-owned flash drive on the promise that he will bring it back
    D. Direct him to the nearest computer/retail store to purchase the flash drive

24. If people call for a Town Hall meeting, which of the following would NOT be a good reason to hold one? 24.____
    A. To voice a common concern shared by members of the community
    B. To present a new proposal that impacts the public
    C. To settle a dispute between rival advisors at City Hall
    D. To collect feedback in response to a new rule or policy implementation

25. Of the following Town Hall meeting pitfalls, which would MOST leave residents feeling as though they wasted their time? 25.____
    A. Not participative or interactive
    B. Poorly designed PowerPoint or on-screen presentation
    C. Poor time management
    D. Meaningless or irrelevant content

KEY (CORRECT ANSWERS)

1. D
2. A
3. C
4. B
5. C

6. A
7. D
8. B
9. B
10. C

11. A
12. C
13. D
14. A
15. B

16. D
17. C
18. D
19. B
20. A

21. C
22. B
23. A
24. C
25. D

EXAMINATION SECTION

TEST 1

DIRECTIONS: Each question or incomplete statement is followed by several suggested answers or completions. Select the one that BEST answers the question or completes the statement. *PRINT THE LETTER OF THE CORRECT ANSWER IN THE SPACE AT THE RIGHT.*

1. A woman in her mid-30s comes up to your desk and asks you how she can apply to work at your office. You do not know the immediate answer to that question. 1.____
   Which of the following would be the BEST way to respond to her request?
   A. Tell her what sounds like the right answer
   B. Tell her to talk to your boss and show her how to do that
   C. Explain you are not allowed to give out confidential information to the public
   D. Inform her that you do not know right now, but you will find out

2. A person approaches the customer service desk and asks you to do something that you are ultimately unable to do. 2.____
   Which of the following should you avoid doing next?
   A. Opening your policy handbook and reading from it verbatim
   B. Clarifying why you cannot do what he or she is asking of you
   C. Crafting detailed and precise statements
   D. Giving the person alternative options

3. When talking to someone from the public, which of the following statements would be LEAST frustrating for the customer to hear? 3.____
   A. "You'll have to..."
   B. "Mr. X will be back at any moment..."
   C. "Let me see what I can do..."
   D. "I'll do my best..."

4. Your office recently received a letter from an individual expressing extreme frustration and disappointment at how it was handling the customer's problems. You have written an apology letter and are reviewing it before sending it to the customer. 4.____
   You should ensure the letter is NOT
   A. sincere
   B. official
   C. personal
   D. sent immediately

5. If you are unable to provide a certain service or product with dependability and accuracy, it would be defined as a lack of 5.____
   A. courtesy
   B. reliability
   C. assurance
   D. responsiveness

6. As most civil service employees know, customer feedback can be, and usually is, an integral part of customer service. Which of the following feedback scenarios would be MOST useful to your organization? 6.____
   A. When it is an ongoing feedback system
   B. When centered on internal customers
   C. When it is focused on only a few indicators
   D. When every employee can see the feedback coming in

7. Which of the following is the LEAST important factor in making sure a customer survey is a valuable tool for your company? 7.____
   A. Taking every precaution to ensure the survey input is maintained in a confidential manner
   B. Making sure the customers believe in the confidentiality of the survey
   C. Ensuring confidentiality by having an outside company administer the survey
   D. Making sure the employees buy in and promote the survey to customers

8. Which of the following would NOT be considered part of the resolution process when identifying and dealing with a customers' problems? 8.____
   A. Following up with the customer after resolving the issue
   B. Listening and responding to each complaint the customer registers
   C. Giving the customer what they originally requested
   D. Promising the customer whatever you need to

9. A customer approaches you with a complaint. You want to arrive at a fair solution to the problem. What is the FIRST step you should take in this situation? 9.____
   A. Immediately defend your company from any customer criticisms
   B. Listen to the customer describe their problem
   C. Ask the customer questions to confirm the type of problem they are having
   D. Determine a solution to the customer's problem(s)

10. If you are dealing with a customer in a prompt manner when addressing their complaints or issues, which of the following are you demonstrating? 10.____
   A. Assurance
   B. Empathy
   C. Responsiveness
   D. Reliability

11. Steve has recently been hired to work at the postal office in town. A customer comes into the office to complain about the number of packages of his they have lost over the past year. When Steve attempts to help the upset customer, what should he make sure to do FIRST? He should 11.____
   A. check into how legitimate the customer's complaints are and see if he can do anything about the missing packages
   B. just let the customer blow off some steam and chalk it up to an emotional outburst

C. ask for help from his boss to see how to handle the situation
D. assume the complaints are accurate and immediately attempt to correct them

12. How should a service representative react when a customer first presents them with a request? 12.____
A. Apologize
B. Greet them in a friendly manner
C. Read from the employee handbook about the request
D. Ask the customer to clarify information

13. In order to assuage a customer's frustration, which of the following should a civil service employee demonstrate? 13.____
A. Urgency B. Indifference C. Surprise D. Compassion

14. A customer comes into the office requesting that your organization do something for them that you know is not part of organization policy. 14.____
Your FIRST responsibility would be to
A. pass the customer on to higher management to deal with the issue
B. persuade the customer to believe that the organization can grant their request
C. mold expectations so they more closely resemble what the organization can do for the customer
D. tell the customer there is no way you can comply with their request

15. Of the following potential distractors, which one MOST prevents a civil service employee from displaying good listening skills while a customer is speaking? 15.____
A. Cell phones or checking e-mail
B. Asking superfluous questions
C. Background office noise
D. Interrupting the customer to speak with colleagues

16. If you are in a situation where you have to deliver a negative response to a customer, it is often better to say _____ instead of just saying "no"? 16.____
A. "I will try to..." B. "You can..."
C. "Our policy does not allow..." D. "I do not believe..."

17. You are working one-on-one with a customer. 17.____
Which of the following would be the MOST appropriate body language to display?
A. Make frowning faces
B. Stare at a spot over the customer's shoulder
C. Lean in toward the customer
D. Cross your arms while they speak

18. The majority of communication in face-to-face meetings with customers is shown through 18.____
A. word choice B. tone
C. clothing choice D. body language

19. A customer angrily approaches you at your service desk and starts expressing his frustration with recent actions by your department. 19.____
Which of the following should be your FIRST responses to the customer?
   A. Listen to the person, then express understanding and apologize for how they have been negatively affected by your department's action
   B. Interrupt them while they are speaking and tell them to calm down or you will not help them
   C. Give them an explanation of why your department took the actions they did
   D. None of the above

20. Of the following services, which one is NOT customized to a specific individual's needs? 20.____
   A. Hair salon
   B. Elementary education
   C. Computer counseling
   D. Dental care

21. Which of the following civil service employees demonstrates excellent customer service? 21.____
   A. A park ranger who minimizes public interaction and contact
   B. The Postal Service employee who sees the customer as a commodity
   C. The office clerk who spends a lot of time with customers sharing personal stories and anecdotes
   D. A DMV employee with open body language and direct communication

22. It is important to have excellent knowledge of services and products, if applicable, when interacting with consumers because 22.____
   A. you can demonstrate your knowledge and impress the customer
   B. your organization can have a higher margin of profit regardless of customer benefit
   C. the customer's needs can best be matched with appropriate services/products
   D. you can look good to your superiors and keep your job

23. A park ranger has recently been coming to a kids' camp dirty and unkempt. Even though her job requires her to be outside at ties, why should she still care about her personal appearance? 23.____
   A. To speed up her service to the public
   B. So she is seen as a professional in her field
   C. It would help her organizational skills
   D. To show her level of expertise as a park ranger

24. How could guided conversation be a positive with interacting with the public? 24.____
   A. It allows you to anticipate a person's needs and expectations.
   B. Most people know what they want even before they show up to your office.
   C. It creates the impression of friendliness.
   D. It helps time move faster.

25. In the event a conflict or crisis arises, which of the following would be considered a POOR action to take when interacting with the public? 25.____
   A. Provide a constant flow of information
   B. Put the public's needs first
   C. Avoid saying "No Comment" as much as possible
   D. Assign multiple spokespeople so media calls can be dealt with efficiently

KEY (CORRECT ANSWERS)

1. D
2. A
3. C
4. B
5. B

6. A
7. C
8. D
9. B
10. C

11. A
12. D
13. A
14. C
15. D

16. B
17. C
18. D
19. A
20. B

21. D
22. C
23. B
24. A
25. D

TEST 2

DIRECTIONS: Each question or incomplete statement is followed by several suggested answers or completions. Select the one that BEST answers the question or completes the statement. *PRINT THE LETTER OF THE CORRECT ANSWER IN THE SPACE AT THE RIGHT.*

1. John Smith answers a caller who struggles to understand a convoluted policy of your agency. 1.____
   How should he handle the customer's question?
   A. Tell the caller to go to the agency's website
   B. He should be honest and say he does not know the answer to the question
   C. John should explain the policy in general terms and refer them to a written version of the policy
   D. Tell the caller to talk to his supervisor and then give the caller the supervisor's extension

2. While meeting with a group of young campers at the local parks and recreation office, you conduct a lecture on the importance of avoiding dangerous plants near the forest. 2.____
   What can you do to make sure your inexperienced audience remembers the main points of your presentation?
   A. Use flashy visuals that catch the eye
   B. Repeat and emphasize your points
   C. Make jokes so the presentation is livelier
   D. Allow the campers to ask questions at the end of the presentation

3. A park ranger is about to deliver a speech at a public conservation meeting. 3.____
   Which of the following is the MOST important thing to keep in mind as he preps for the presentation?
   A. How large the audience is
   B. Whether or not he will be able to use visual aids
   C. If he will have time to use charts and graphs
   D. Audience interests

4. Jerry receives a letter from a customer and is about to shred it without reading. 4.____
   When you stop him, he says that there is no reason to read it because you cannot learn very much from letters you receive from the public.
   Which of the following should you tell him in order to convince him that reading letters sent from the public is beneficial and necessary?
   A. These public letters can give us a feel for how we are meeting customer needs.
   B. Letters from the public tell us how well our informational efforts are working.
   C. These letters can inform us of what additional training we may need.
   D. The letters can tell us whether public information processes need to be changed or not.

5. Mary Jane is a volunteer with the Parks and Recreation Department and her children also attend various summer programs through the district. She comes to you today to complain that one of her children was not allowed to join a program because they missed the sign-up by one day. She calls your staff a bunch of "morons" and complains that your department's actions are creating serious issues for her. 5.____
How should you handle this situation?
   A. Let Ms. Johnson rant until she gets it out of her system
   B. Tell her you cannot help her and will ask her to leave if she cannot stop referring to your colleagues as "morons"
   C. Refer Ms. Johnson to your boss
   D. Try to alter the tone of the conversation to a more objective and less emotional discussion of Ms. Johnson's problems

6. A civil service employee is tasked with moderating a town hall meeting regarding child safety, but he knows that residents will be attending the meeting with different motives. 6.____
How can the employee make sure the town hall meeting is as beneficial and informational as possible?
   A. Ask attendees to be open to changing their opinions and preferences
   B. Start out by recognizing the various motives but also stress the common objectives and interests
   C. Call out individuals who you know have specific reasons for attending and put them on the spot
   D. Cancel the meeting and avoid rescheduling it until you can be sure everyone is on the same page

7. During the question-and-answer session at the end of a presentation, a member of the public makes a suggestion that you deem not only practical but worthy of further discussion. 7.____
How should you react to this?
   A. Tell them you will let the appropriate people know of the suggestion
   B. Tell the person you concur with them wholeheartedly
   C. Let the person know you think it is a good idea but you cannot make decisions based on suggestions during Q and A
   D. Even though the suggestion is good, tell the person that someone in your organization has probably already thought of the idea

8. When in a conversation with a group of local residents, what is the BIGGEST problem with one or two people dominating the conversation? 8.____
   A. Your interaction could take longer than it should
   B. Some people will become distracted and not focus on the meeting anymore
   C. The other member of the group may not have an opportunity to share their opinions
   D. None of the above

9. You receive a phone call at the village hall, but the information being requested would need to come from the police station.
How should you respond to the caller? 9.____
A. Give them the police station's website and wish them well
B. Tell them you are not responsible for their request
C. Refer them to the police station's number and information
D. Provide them with the information as best as you can

10. Which of the following should almost always be avoided when interacting with a member of the community? 10.____
A. Contentious matters
B. Topics about financial material
C. Rules and regulations
D. Technical lingo or jargon

11. When people use inflammatory language laced with obscenities, a town employee should 11.____
A. refuse to continue the dialogue if the person cannot stop using the offensive language
B. tell the person to talk to your supervisor
C. allow the person to finish "venting" before attempting to find a solution to the problem
D. hang up if on the phone; if in person, leave the area and ask the individual to leave as well

12. A member of the public has sent your agency a letter.
Which of the following will help you figure out how much explaining you need to do when writing a response? 12.____
A. Go to the agency website and search for how much explanation is provided there
B. Take out the original customer letter and study it
C. Presume the person who wrote the letter already has a working knowledge of the subject and thus will not require a lot of background explanation
D. Look at past letters sent by your agency

13. During an informational meeting with local townspeople, a man makes a suggestion for a new town measure that is based on incorrect information and is impractical.
What is the BEST way to handle a situation such as this? 13.____
A. Ask if anyone else in attendance would like to respond to the suggestion
B. Tell the person it is a great idea even though you are aware of its folly
C. Thank the man for coming and tell everyone you always welcome their suggestions
D. Inform the person that his/her comment clearly reflects an inferior knowledge about the subject

14. A member from the public calls your office about negative comments he has heard about one of your programs. You believe the comments were made by someone who had inaccurate material, but you are not completely certain of that because you are not directly involved with the program. 14.____

What is the BEST way to handle this situation?

A. Tell the caller you will analyze the situation in depth and then call them back
B. Tell the caller the evidence on which they have based their judgment is not supported
C. Explain that your office has a "No Comment" policy regarding negative comments
D. Let the caller know you are not involved with the program directly, and tell them to call the person who is

15. Which of the following quotes reflects the BEST way to handle an angry resident that keeps interrupting during a village meeting? 15.____

A. "I am here as a volunteer and I do not need this."
B. "I understand your anger, but we have quite a bit of information to cover tonight, so in fairness to everyone else, please let me continue."
C. "Every crowd has one black sheep in it."
D. "Sir, (or Ma'am) if you cannot stop interjecting, I will have security escort you from the premises."

16. Of the following, which is an example of nonverbal communication? 16.____

A. Frowning
B. Hand signs
C. A "21 Gun Salute"
D. All of the above

17. Residents of Masterton, Georgia, were recently made aware that the main road into and out of town will be under construction for the next four years. The construction will make travel time much more difficult for the citizens and they have demanded a meeting with your department. You are tasked with creating a presentation to explain to them why the construction is necessary. 17.____
At the start of the presentation, you should

A. make a joke to lighten the mood
B. state the purpose of your presentation
C. provide a detailed account of the history behind the project
D. make a call to action

18. When a member of the public asks questions that are confusing or you do not understand right away, what is the BEST way to handle this situation? 18.____

A. Answer the question as you understand it
B. Stick to generalizations dealing with the subject of the question
C. Rephrase the question and ask the person if you understood what they were asking
D. Ask the person to repeat the question

19. When preparing for a public interaction, which of the following situations would be MOST appropriate to include handouts? 19.____

A. If you want to help the attendees remember important information after the interaction is over
B. If you want to keep the interaction short

C. When you want to remember key points to talk about
D. When you do not want attendees to have to pay attention during the interaction

20. John is in the process of handling a phone call when a local citizen approaches his desk to ask a question. Neither the caller nor the visitor seem to be in a crisis. 20.____
What should John do in this scenario?
A. Keep talking with the caller until he is finished. Then tell the visitor he is sorry for making them wait.
B. Remain on the phone with the caller but look up at the visitor every once and awhile so they know he has not forgotten about them.
C. Tell the caller he has a visitor, so the conversation needs to end.
D. Tell the visitor he will be with them as soon as he finishes the phone call.

21. When engaged in conversation with another person, which communication technique is MOST likely to ensure you comprehend fully what the other person to trying to communicate to you? 21.____
A. Repeat back to the person what you think they are communicating
B. Continual eye contact
C. Making sure the person speaks slowly
D. Nodding your head while they speak

22. You encounter someone who is frustrated about a situation and needs to vent by talking it out before they can move onto a productive conversation. 23.____
When a situation is like this, it is often BEST to
A. recommend various strategies for calming down
B. Ask to be excused from the conversation without offering why
C. Explain to the person that it is unproductive to behave the way they are currently behaving
D. Acknowledge that venting is a crucial step to moving past the emotions and allow the person to express his or her feelings

23. Which of the following is NOT an example of active listening? 23.____
A. Taking notes
B. Referring the customer to the manager after they are done speaking
C. Using phrases like "I see" or "Go on"
D. Repeating back to the customer what you've heard

24. Which of the following questions would be classified as a clarification question? 24.____
A. "How long have you sold spoiled meat?"
B. "Do you like our brand?"
C. "You mentioned you liked this merchandise. How would you feel about this?"
D. None of the above

25. When interacting with a member of the public, which of the following words should you avoid using as it is not positive as perceived by most people? 25.____
    A. "Absolutely"
    B. "You are welcome"
    C. "Here's what I can do"
    D. "I'll do my best"

KEY (CORRECT ANSWERS)

1. C
2. B
3. D
4. A
5. D

6. B
7. A
8. C
9. C
10. D

11. A
12. B
13. C
14. A
15. B

16. D
17. B
18. C
19. A
20. D

21. A
22. D
23. B
24. C
25. D

LOGICAL REASONING
EVALUATING CONCLUSIONS IN LIGHT OF KNOWN FACTS

EXAMINATION SECTION

TEST 1

COMMENTARY

This section is designed to provide practice questions in evaluating conclusions when you are given specific data to work with.

We suggest you do the questions three at a time, consulting the answer key and then the solution section for any questions you may have missed. It's a good idea to try the questions again a week before the exam.

In the validity of conclusion type of question, you are first given a reading passage which describes a particular situation. The passage may be on any topic, as it is not your knowledge of the topic that is being tested, but your reasoning abilities. The passage is likely to detail several proposed courses of action and factors affecting these proposals. The reading passage is followed by a conclusion based on the facts in the passage, or a description of a decision taken regarding the situation. The conclusion is followed by a number of statements which have a possible connection to the conclusion. For each statement, you are to determine whether:

A. The statement proves the conclusion.
B. The statement supports the conclusion but does not prove it.
C. The statement disproves the conclusion.
D. The statement weakens the conclusion but does not disprove it.
E. The statement has no relevance to the conclusion.

Remember that the conclusion after the passage is to be accepted as the outcome of what actually happened, and that you are being asked to evaluate the impact each statement would have had on the conclusion.

Questions 1-8.

DIRECTIONS: Questions 1 through 8 are based on the following paragraph.

In May of 2018, Mr. Bryan inherited a clothing store on Main Street in a small New England town. The store has specialized in selling quality men's and women's clothing since 1920. Business has been stable throughout the years, neither increasing nor decreasing. He has an opportunity to buy two adjacent stores which would enable him to add a wider range and style of clothing. In order to do this, he would have to borrow a substantial amount of money. He also risks losing the goodwill of his present clientele.

CONCLUSION: On November 7, 2018, Mr. Bryan tells the owner of the two adjacent stores that he has decided not to purchase them. He feels that it would be best to simply maintain his present marketing position, as there would not be enough new business to support an expansion.

A. The statement proves the conclusion.
B. The statement supports the conclusion but does not prove it.
C. The statement disproves the conclusion.
D. The statement weakens the conclusion.
E. The statement is irrelevant to the conclusion.

1. A large new branch of the county's community college holds its first classes in September. 1.____

2. The town's largest factory shuts down with no indication that it will reopen. 2.____

3. The United States Census showed that the number of children per household dropped from 2.4 to 2.1 since the last census. 3.____

4. Mr. Bryan's brother tells him of a new clothing boutique specializing in casual women's clothing which is opening soon. 4.____

5. Mr. Bryan's sister buys her baby several items for Christmas at Mr. Bryan's store. 5.____

6. Mrs. McIntyre, the President of the Town Council, brings Mr. Bryan a home-baked pumpkin pie in honor of his store's 100th anniversary. They discuss the changes that have taken place in the town, and she comments on how his store has maintained the same look and feel over the years. 6.____

7. In October, Mr. Bryan's aunt lends him $50,000. 7.____

8. The Town Council has just announced that the town is eligible for funding from a federal project designed to encourage the location of new businesses in the central districts of cities and towns. 8.____

Questions 9-18.

DIRECTIONS: Questions 9 through 18 are based on the following paragraph.

A proposal was put before the legislative body of a country to require air bags in all automobiles manufactured for domestic use in that country after 2019. The air bag, made of nylon or plastic, is designed to inflate automatically within a car at the impact of a collision, thus protecting front-seat occupants from being thrown forward. There has been much support of the measure from consumer groups, the insurance industry, key legislators, and the general public. The country's automobile manufacturers, who contend the new crash equipment would add up to $1,000 to car prices and provide no more protection than existing seat belts, are against the proposed legislation

CONCLUSION: On April 21, 2014, the legislation requiring air bags in all automobiles manufactured for domestic use in that country after 2019.

A. The statement proves the conclusion.
B. The statement supports the conclusion but does not prove it.
C. The statement disproves the conclusion.
D. The statement weakens the conclusion.
E. The statement is irrelevant to the conclusion.

9. A study has shown that 59% of car occupants do not use seat belts. 9.____

10. The country's Department of Transportation has estimated that the crash protection equipment would save up to 5,900 lives each year. 10.____

11. On April 27, 2013, Augusta Raneoni was named head of an advisory committee to gather and analyze data on the costs, benefits, and feasibility of the proposed legislation on air bags in automobiles. 11.____

12. Consumer groups and the insurance industry accuse the legislature of rejecting passage of the regulation for political reasons. 12.____

13. A study by the Committee on Imports and Exports projected that the sales of imported cars would rise dramatically in 2019 because imported cars do not have to include air bags, and can be sold more cheaply. 13.____

14. Research has shown that air bags, if produced on a large scale, would cost about $200 apiece, and would provide more reliable protection than any other type of seat belt. 14.____

15. Auto sales in 2011 increased 3% over the previous year. 15.____

16. A Department of Transportation report in July of 2020 credits a drop in automobile deaths of 4,100 to the use of air bags. 16.____

17. In June of 2014, the lobbyist of the largest insurance company receives a bonus for her work on the passage of the air bag legislation. 17.____

18. In 2020, the stock in crash protection equipment has risen three-fold over the previous year. 18.____

Questions 19-25.

DIRECTIONS: Questions 19 through 25 are based on the following paragraph.

On a national television talk show, Joan Rivera, a famous comedienne, has recently insulted the physical appearances of a famous actress and the dead wife of an ex-President. There has been a flurry of controversy over her comments, and much discussion of the incident has appeared in the press. Most of the comments have been negative. It appears that this tie she might have gone too far. There have been cancellations of two of her five scheduled performances in the two weeks since the show was televised, and Joan's been receiving a lot of negative mail. Because of the controversy, she has an interview with a national news magazine at the end of the week, and her press agent is strongly urging her to apologize publicly. She feels strongly that her comments were no worse than any other she has ever made, and that the whole incident will *blow over* soon. She respects her press agent's judgment, however, as his assessment of public sentiment tends to be very accurate.

CONCLUSION: Joan does not apologize publicly, and during the interview she challenges the actress to a weight-losing contest. For every pound the actress loses, Joan says she will donate $1 to the Cellulite Prevention League.

A. The statement proves the conclusion.
B. The statement supports the conclusion but does not prove it.
C. The statement disproves the conclusion.
D. The statement weakens the conclusion.
E. The statement is irrelevant to the conclusion.

19. Joan's mother, who she is very fond of, is very upset with Joan's comments. 19.____

20. Six months after the interview, Joan's income has doubled. 20.____

21. Joan's agent is pleased with the way Joan handles the interview. 21.____

22. Joan's sister has been appointed Treasurer of the Cellulite Prevention League In her report, she states that Joan's $12 contribution is the only amount that has been donated to the League in its first six months. 22.____

23. The magazine receives many letters commending Joan for the courage it took for her to apologize publicly in the interview. 23.____

24. Immediately after the interview appears, another one of Joan's performances is cancelled. 24.____

25. Due to a printers' strike, the article was not published until the following week. 25.____

Questions 26-30.

DIRECTIONS: Questions 25 through 30 are based on the following paragraph.

The law-making body of Country X must decide what to do about the issue of recording television shows for home use. There is currently no law against recording shows directly from the TV as long as the DVDs are not used for commercial purposes. The increasing popularity of pay TV and satellite systems, combined with the increasing number of homes that own recording equipment, has caused a great deal of concern in some segments of the entertainment industry. Companies that own the rights to films, popular television shows, and sporting events feel that their copyright privileges are being violated, and they are seeking compensation or the banning of TV recording. Legislation has been introduced to make it illegal to record television programs for home use. Separate proposed legislation is also pending that would continue to allow recording of TV shows for home use, but would place a tax of 10% on each DVD that is purchased for home use. The income from that tax would then be proportionately distributed as royalties to those owning the rights to programs being aired. A weighted point system coupled with the averaging of several national viewing rating systems would be used to determine the royalties. There is a great deal of lobbying being done for both bills, as the manufacturers of DVDs and recording equipment are against the passage of the bills.

CONCLUSION: The legislature of Country X rejects both bills by a wide margin.

A. The statement proves the conclusion.
B. The statement supports the conclusion but does not prove it.
C. The statement disproves the conclusion.
D. The statement weakens the conclusion.
E. The statement is irrelevant to the conclusion.

26. Country X's Department of Taxation hires 500 new employees to handle the increased paperwork created by the new tax on DVDs. 26.____

27. A study conducted by the country's most prestigious accounting firm shows that the cost of implementing the proposed new DVD tax would be greater than the income expected from it. 27.____

28. It is estimated that 80% of all those working in the entertainment industry, excluding performers, own DVD recorders. 28.____

29. The head of Country X's law enforcement agency states that legislation banning the home recording of TV shows would be unenforceable. 29.____

30. Financial experts predict that unless a tax is placed on DVDs, several large companies in the entertainment industry will have to file for bankruptcy. 30.____

Questions 31-38.

DIRECTIONS: Questions 31 through 38 are variations on the type of question you just had. It is important that you read the question very carefully to determine exactly what is required.

31. In this question, select the choice that is MOST relevant to the conclusion. 31.____
I. The Buffalo Bills football team is in second place in its division.
II. The New England Patriots are in first place in the same division.
III. There are two games left to play in the season, and the Bills will not play the Patriots again.
IV. The New England Patriots won ten games and lost four games, and the Buffalo Bills have won eight games and lost six games.
CONCLUSION: The Buffalo Bills win their division.
A. The conclusion is proved by sentences I-IV.
B. The conclusion is disproved by sentences I-IV.
C. The facts are not sufficient to prove or disprove the conclusion.

32. In this question, select the choice that is MOST relevant to the conclusion. 32.____
I. On the planet of Zeinon there are only two different eye colors and only two different hair colors.
II. Half of those beings with purple hair have golden eyes.
III. There are more inhabitants with purple hair than there are inhabitants with silver hair.
IV. One-third of those with silver hair have green eyes.
CONCLUSION: There are more golden-eyed beings on Zeinon than green-eyed ones.
A. The conclusion is proved by sentences I-IV.
B. The conclusion is disproved by sentences I-IV.
C. The facts are not sufficient to prove or disprove the conclusion.

33. In this question, select the choice that is MOST relevant to the conclusion. 33.____
John and Kevin are leaving Amaranth to go to school in Bethany. They've decided to rent a small truck to move their possessions. Joe's Truck Rental charges $100 plus 30¢ a mile. National Movers charges $50 more but gives free mileage for the first 100 miles. After the first 100 miles, they charge 25¢ a mile.
CONCLUSION: John and Kevin rent their truck from National Movers because it is cheaper.
A. The conclusion is proved by the facts in the above paragraph.
B. The conclusion is disproved by the facts in the above paragraph.
C. The facts are not sufficient to prove or disprove the conclusion.

34. For this question, select the choice that supports the information given in the passage. 34.____

Municipalities in Country X are divided into villages, towns, and cities. A village has a population of 5,000 or less. The population of a town ranges from 5,001 to 15,000. In order to be incorporated as a city, the municipality must have a population over 15,000. If, after a village becomes a town, or a town becomes a city, the population drops below the minimum required (for example, the population of a city goes below 15,000), and stays below the minimum for more than ten years, it loses its current status, and drops to the next category. As soon as a municipality rises in population to the next category (village to town, for example), however, it is immediately reclassified to the next category.

In the 2000 census, Plainfield had a population of 12,000. Between 2000 and 2010, Plainfield grew 10%, and between 2010 and 2020 Plainfield grew another 20%. The population of Springdale doubled from 2000 to 2010, and increased 25% from 2010 to 2020. The city of Smallville's population, 20,283, has not changed significantly in recent years. Granton had a population of 25,000 people in1990, and has decreased 25% in each ten year period since then. Ellenville had a population of 4,283 in 1990, and grew 5% in each ten year period since 1990.

In 2020,

A. Plainfield, Smallville, and Granton are cities.
B. Smallville is a city, Granton is a town, and Ellenville is a village.
C. Springdale, Granton, and Ellenville are towns.
D. Plainfield and Smallville are cities, and Ellenville is a town.

35. For this question, select the choice that is MOST relevant to the conclusion. 35.____

A study was done for a major food-distributing firm to determine if there is any difference in the kind of caffeine containing products used by people of different ages. A sample of one thousand people between the ages of twenty and fifty were drawn from selected areas in the country. They were divided equally into three groups.

Those individuals who were 20-29 were designated Group A, those 30-39 were Group B, and those 40-50 were placed in Group C.

It was found that on the average, Group A drank 1.8 cups of coffee, Group B 3.1, and Group C 2.5 cups of coffee daily. Group A drank 2.1 cups of tea, Group B drank 1.2, and Group C drank 2.6 cups of tea daily. Group A drank 3 1.8 ounces glasses of cola, Group B drank 1.9, and Group C drank 1.5 glasses of cola daily.

CONCLUSION: According to the study, the average person in the 20-29 age group drinks less tea daily than the average person in the 40-50 age group, but drinks more coffee daily than the average person in the 30-39 age group drinks cola.

A. The conclusion is proved by the facts in the above paragraph.
B. The conclusion is disproved by the facts in the above paragraph.
C. The facts are not sufficient to prove or disprove the conclusion.

36. For this question, select the choice that is MOST relevant to the conclusion 36.____

I. Mary is taller than Jane but shorter than Dale.
II. Fred is taller than Mary but shorter than Steven.
III. Dale is shorter than Steven but taller than Elizabeth.
IV. Elizabeth is taller than Mary but not as tall as Fred.

CONCLUSION: Dale is taller than Fred.

A. The conclusion is proved by sentences I-IV.
B. The conclusion is disproved by sentences I-IV.
C. The facts are not sufficient to prove or disprove the conclusion.

37. For this question, select the choice that is MOST relevant to the conclusion. 37.____

I. Main Street is between Spring Street and Glenn Blvd.
II. Hawley Avenue is one block south of Spring Street and three blocks north of Main Street.
III. Glenn Street is five blocks south of Elm and four blocks south of Main.
IV. All the streets mentioned are parallel to one another.

CONCLUSION: Elm Street is between Hawley Avenue and Glenn Blvd.

A. The conclusion is proved by the facts in sentences I-IV.
B. The conclusion is disproved by the facts in sentences I-IV.
C. The facts are not sufficient to prove or disprove the conclusion.

38. For this question, select the choice that is MOST relevant to the conclusion. 38.____
I. Train A leaves the town of Hampshire every day at 5:50 A.M. and arrives in New London at 6:42 A.M.
II. Train A leaves New London at 7:00 A.M. and arrives in Kellogsville at 8:42 A.M.
III. Train B leaves Kellogsville at 8:00 A.M. and arrives in Hampshire at 10:45 A.M.
IV. Due to the need for repairs, there is just one railroad track between New London and Hampshire.
CONCLUSION: It is impossible for Train A and Train B to follow these schedules without colliding.
A. The conclusion is proved by the facts in sentences I-IV.
B. The conclusion is disproved by the facts in sentences I-IV.
C. The facts are not sufficient to prove or disprove the conclusion.

KEY (CORRECT ANSWERS)

1.	D	11.	C	21.	D	31.	C
2.	B	12.	C	22.	A	32.	A
3.	E	13.	D	23.	C	33.	C
4.	B	14.	B	24.	B	34.	B
5.	C	15.	E	25.	E	35.	B
6.	A	16.	B	26.	C	36.	C
7.	D	17.	A	27.	B	37.	A
8.	B	18.	B	28.	E	38.	B
9.	B	19.	D	29.	B		
10.	B	20.	E	30.	D		

SOLUTIONS TO QUESTIONS

1. The answer is D. This statement weakens the conclusion, but does not disprove it. If a new branch of the community college opened in September, it could possibly bring in new business for Mr. Bryant. Since it states in the conclusion that Mr. Bryant felt there would not be enough new business to support the additional stores, this would tend to disprove the conclusion. Choice C would not be correct because it's possible that he felt that the students would not have enough additional money to support his new venture, or would not be interested in his clothing styles. It's also possible that the majority of the students already live in the area, so that they wouldn't really be a new customer population. This type of question is tricky, and can initially be very confusing, so don't feel badly if you missed it. Most people need to practice with a few of these types of questions before they feel comfortable recognizing exactly what they're being asked to do.

2. The answer is B. It supports the conclusion because the closing of the factory would probably take money and customers out of the town, causing Mr. Bryant to lose some of his present business. It doesn't prove the conclusion, however, because we don't know how large the factory was. It's possible that only a small percentage of the population was employed there, or that they found other jobs.

3. The answer is E. The fact that the number of children per household dropped slightly nationwide in the decade is irrelevant. Statistics showing a drop nationwide doesn't mean that there was a drop in the number of children per household in Mr. Bryant's hometown. This is a tricky question, as choice B, supporting the conclusion but not proving it, may seem reasonable. If the number of children per household declined nationwide, then it may not seem unreasonable to feel that this would support Mr. Bryant's decision not to expand his business. However, we're preparing you for promotional exams, not "real life." One of the difficult things about taking exams is that sometimes you're forced to make a choice between two statements that both seem like they could be the possible answer. What you need to do in that case is choose the best choice. Becoming annoyed or frustrated with the question won't really help much. If there's a review of the exam, you can certainly appeal the question. There have been many cases where, after an appeal, two possible choices have been allowed as correct answers. We've included this question, however, to help you see what to do should you get a question like this. It's most important not to get rattled, and to select the BEST choice. In this case, the connection between the statistical information and Mr. Bryant's decision is pretty remote. If the question had said that the number of children in Mr. Bryant's town had decreased, then choice B would have been a more reasonable choice. It could also help in this situation to visualize the situation. Picture Mr. Bryant in his armchair reading that, nationwide, the average number of children per household has declined slightly. How likely would this be to influence his decision, especially since he sells men's and women's clothing? It would take a while for this decline in population to show up, and we're not even sure if it applies to Mr. Bryant's hometown. Don't feel badly if you missed this; it was tricky. The more of these you do, the more comfortable you'll feel.

4. The answer is B. If a new clothing boutique specializing in casual women's clothing were to open soon, this would lend support to Mr. Bryant's decision not to expand, but would not prove that he had actually made the decision to expand. A new women's clothing boutique would most likely be in competition with his existing business, thus making any possible expansion a riskier venture. We can't be sure from this, however, that he didn't go ahead and expand his business despite the increased competition. Choice A, proves the conclusion, would only be the answer if we could be absolutely sure from the statement that Mr. Bryant had actually not expanded his business.

5. The answer is C. This statement disproves the conclusion. In order for his sister to buy several items for her baby at Mr. Bryant's store, he would have to have changed his business to include children's clothing.

6. The answer is A. It definitely proves the conclusion. The passage states that Mr. Bryan's store had been in business since 1920. A pie baked in honor of his store's 100th anniversary would have to be presented sometime in 2020. The conclusion states that he made his decision not to expand on November 7, 2018. If, more than a year later Mrs. MacIntyre comments that his store has maintained the same look and feel over the years, it could not have been expanded, or otherwise significantly changed.

7. The answer is D. If Mr. Bryant's aunt lent him $50,000 in October, this would tend to weaken the conclusion, which took place in November. Because it was stated that Mr. Bryant would need to borrow money in order to expand his business, it would be logical to assume that if he borrowed money he had decided to expand his business, weakening the conclusion. The reason C, disproves the conclusion, is not the correct answer is because we can't be sure Mr. Bryant didn't borrow the money for another reason.

8. The answer is B. If Mr. Bryant's town is eligible for federal funds to encourage the location of new businesses in the central district, this would tend to support his decision not to expand his business. Funds to encourage new business would increase the likelihood of there being additional competition for Mr. Bryant's store to contend with. Since we can't say for sure that there would be direct competition from a new business, however, choice A would be incorrect. Note that this is also a tricky question. You might have thought that the new funds weakened the conclusion because it would mean that Mr. Bryant could easily get the money he needed. Mr. Bryant is expanding his present business, not creating a new business. Therefore, he is not eligible for the funding.

9. The answer is B. This is a very tricky question. It's stated that 59% of car occupants don't use seat belts. The legislature is considering the use of air bags because of safety issues. The advantage of air bags over seat belts is that they inflate upon impact, and don't require car occupants to do anything with them ahead of time. Since the population has strongly resisted using seat belts, the air bags could become even more important in saving lives. Since saving lives is the purpose of the proposed legislation, the information that a small percentage of people use seat belts could be helpful to the passage of the legislation. We can't be sure that this is reason enough for the legislature to vote for the legislation, however, so choice A in incorrect.

11 (#1)

10. The answer is B, as the information that 5,900 lives could be saved would tend to support the conclusion. Saving that many lives through the use of air bags could be a very persuasive reason to vote for the legislation. Since we don't know for sure that it's enough of a compelling reason for the legislature to vote for the legislation, however, choice A could not be the answer.

11. The answer is C, disproves the conclusion. If the legislation had been passed as stated in the conclusion, there would be no reason to appoint someone head of an advisory committee six days later to analyze the "feasibility of the proposed legislation." The key word here is "proposed." If it has been proposed, it means it hasn't been passed. This contradicts the conclusion and, therefore, disproves it.

12. The answer is C, disproves the conclusion. If the legislation had passed, there would be no reason for supporters of the legislation to accuse the legislature of rejecting the legislation for political reasons. This question may have seemed so obvious that you might have thought there was a trick to it. Exams usually have a few obvious questions, which will trip you up if you begin reading too much into them.

13. The answer is D, as this would tend to disprove the conclusion. A projected dramatic rise in imported cars could be very harmful to the country's economy and could be a very good reason for some legislators to vote against the proposed legislation. It would be assuming too much to choose C, however, because we don't know if they actually did vote against it.

14. The answer is B. This information would tend to support the passage of the legislation. The estimate of the cost of the air bags is $800 less than the cost estimated by opponents, and it's stated that the protection would be more reliable than any other type of seat belt. Both of these would be good arguments in favor of passing the legislation. Since we don't know for sure, however, how persuasive they actually were, choice A would not be the correct choice.

15. The answer is E, as this is irrelevant information. It really doesn't matter whether auto sales in 2001 have increased slightly over the previous year. If the air bag legislation were to go into effect in 2004, that might make the information somehow more relevant. But the air bag legislation would not take effect until 2009, so the information is irrelevant, since it tells us nothing about the state of the auto industry then.

16. The answer is B, supports the conclusion. This is a tricky question. While at first it might seem to prove the conclusion, we can't be sure that the air bag legislation is responsible for the drop in automobile deaths. It's possible air bags came into popular use without the legislation, or with different legislation. There's no way we can be sure that it was the proposed legislation mandating the use of air bags that was responsible.

17. The answer is A. If, in June of 2009, the lobbyist received a bonus "for her work on the air bag legislation," we can be sure that the legislation passed. This proves the conclusion.

18. The answer is B. This is another tricky question. A three-fold stock increase would strongly suggest that the legislation had been passed, but it's possible that factors other than the air bag legislation caused the increase. Note that the stock is in "crash protection

equipment." Nowhere in the statement does it say air bags. Seat belts, motorcycle helmets, and collapsible bumpers are all crash protection equipment and could have contributed to the increase. This is just another reminder to read carefully because the questions are often designed to mislead you.

19. The answer is D. This would tend to weaken the conclusion because Joan is very fond of her mother and she would not want to upset her unnecessarily. It does not prove it, however, because if Joan strongly feels she is right, she probably wouldn't let her mother's opinion sway her. Choice E would also not be correct, because we cannot assume that Joan's mother's opinion is of so little importance to her as to be considered irrelevant.

20. The answer is E. The statement is irrelevant. We are told that Joan's income has doubled but we are not old why. The phrase "six months after the interview" can be misleading in that it leads us to assume that the increase and the interview are related. Her income could have doubled because she regained her popularity but it could also have come from stocks or some other business venture. Because we are not given any reason for her income doubling, it would be impossible to say whether or not this statement proves or disproves the conclusion. Choice E is the best choice of the five possible choices. One of the problems with promotional exams is that sometimes you need to select a choice you're not crazy about. In this case, "not having enough information to made a determination" would be the best choice. However, that's not an option, so you're forced to work with what you've got. On these exams it's sometimes like voting for President; you have to pick the "lesser of the two evils" or the least awful choice. In this case, the information is more irrelevant to the conclusion than it is anything else.

21. The answer is D, weakens the conclusion. We've been told that Joan's agent feels that she should apologize. If he is pleased with her interview, then it would tend to weaken the conclusion but not disprove it. We can't be sure that he hasn't had a change of heart, or that there weren't other parts of the interview he liked so much that they outweighed her unwillingness to apologize.

22. The answer is A. The conclusion states that Joan will donate $1 to the Cellulite Prevention League for every pound the actress loses. Joan's sister's financial report on the League's activities directly supports and proves the conclusion.

23. The answer is C, disproves the conclusion. If the magazine receives many letters commending Joan for her courage in apologizing, this directly contradicts the conclusion, which states that Joan didn't apologize.

24. The answer is B. It was stated in the passage that two of Joan's performances were cancelled after the controversy first occurred. The cancellation of another performance immediately after her interview was published would tend to support the conclusion that she refused to apologize. Because we can't be sure, however, that her performance wasn't cancelled for another reason, choice A would be incorrect.

25. The answer is E, as this information is irrelevant. Postponing the article an extra week does not affect Joan's decision or the public's reaction to it.

26. The answer is C. If 500 new employees are hired to handle the "increased paperwork created by the new tax on DVDs," this would directly contradict the conclusion, which states that the legislature defeated both bills. (They should all be this easy.)

27. The answer is B. The results of the study would support the conclusion. If implementing the legislation was going to be so costly, it is likely that the legislature would vote against it. Choice A is not the answer, however, because we can't be sure that the legislature didn't pass it anyway.

28. The answer is E. It's irrelevant to the conclusion that 80% of all those working in the entertainment industry own DVD recorders. Sometimes if you're not sure about these, it can help a lot to try and visualize the situation. Why would someone voting on this legislation care about this fact? It doesn't seem to be the kind of information that would make any difference or impact upon the conclusion.

29. The answer is B. The head of the law enforcement agency's statement that the legislation would be unenforceable would support the conclusion. It's possible that many legislators would question why they should bother to pass legislation that would be impossible to enforce. Choice A would be incorrect, however, because we can't be sure that the legislation wasn't passed in spite of his statement.

30. The answer is D. This would tend to weaken the conclusion because the prospect of several large companies going bankrupt would seem to be a good argument in favor of the legislation. The possible loss of jobs and businesses would be a good reason for some people to vote for the legislation. We can't be sure, however, that this would be a competing enough reason to ensure passage of the legislation so choice C is incorrect.

This concludes our section on the "Validity of Conclusion" type of questions. We hope these weren't too horrible for you. It's important to keep in mind <u>exactly</u> what you've been given and <u>exactly</u> what they want you to do with it. It's also necessary to remember that you may have to choose between two possible answers. In that case, you must choose the one that seems the best. Sometimes you may think there is no good answer. You will probably be right, but you can't let that upset you. Just choose the one you dislike the least.

We want to repeat that it is unlikely that this exact format will appear on the exam. The skills required to answer these questions, however, are the same as those you'll need for the exam so we suggest that you review this section before taking the actual exam.

31. The answer is C. This next set of questions requires you to "switch gears" slightly, and get used to different formats. In this type of question, you have to decide whether the conclusion is proved by the facts give, disproved by the facts given, or neither because note enough information has been provided. Fortunately, unlike the previous questions, you don't have to decide whether particular facts support or don't support the conclusion. This type of question is more straight forward, but the reasoning behind it is the same. We are told that the Bills have won two games less than the Patriots, and that the Patriots are in first place and the Bills are in second place. We are also told that there are two games left to play, and that they won't play each other again. The conclusion states that the Bills won the division. Is there anything in the four statements that would prove this? We have

no idea what the outcome of the last two games of the season was. The Bills and Patriots could have ended up tied at the end of the season, or the Bills could have lost both or one of their last games while the Patriots did the same. There might even be another team tied for first or second place with the Bills or Patriots. Since we don't know for sure, Choice A is incorrect. Choice B is trickier. It might seem at first glance that the best the Bills could do would be to tie the Patriots if the Patriots lost their last two games and the Bills won their last two games. But it would be too much to assume that there is no procedure for a tiebreaker that wouldn't give the Bills the division championship. Since we don't know what the rules are in the event of a tie (for example, what if a tie was decided on the results of what happened when the two teams had played each other, or on the best record in the division, or on most points scored?), we can't say for sure that it would be impossible for the Bills to win their division. For this reason, choice C is the answer, as we don't have enough information to prove or disprove the conclusion. This question looked more difficult than it actually was. It's important to disregard any factors outside of the actual question, and to focus only on what you've been given. In this case, as on all of these types of questions, what you know or don't know about a subject is actually irrelevant. It's best to concentrate only on the actual facts given.

32. The answer is A. The conclusion is proved by the facts given.

In this type of problem, it is usually best to pull as many facts as possible from the sentences and then put them into a simpler form. The phrasing and the order of exam questions are designed to be confusing so you need to restate things as clearly as possible by eliminating the extras.

Sentence I tells us that there are only two possible colors for eyes and two for hair. Looking at the other sentences we learn that eyes are either green or gold and that hair is either silver or purple. If half the beings with purple hair have golden eyes, then the other half must have green eyes since it is the only other eye color. Likewise, if one-third of those with silver hair have green eyes, the other two-thirds must have golden eyes.

This information makes it clear that there are more golden-eyed beings on Zeinon than green-eyed ones. It doesn't matter that we don't know exactly how many are actually living on the planet. The number of those with gold eyes (1/2 plus 2/3) will always be greater than the number of those with green eyes (1/2 plus 1/3), no matter what the actual figures might be. Sentence III is totally irrelevant because even if there were more silver-haired inhabitants it would not affect the conclusion.

33. The answer is C. The conclusion is neither proved nor disproved by the facts because we don't know how many miles Bethany is from Amoranth.

With this type of question, if you're not sure how to approach it, you can always substitute in a range of "real numbers" to see what the result would be. If they were 200 miles apart, Joe's Truck Rental would be cheaper because they would charge a total of $160 while National Movers would charge $175.

Joe's - $100 plus .30 x 200 (or $60) = $160
National - $150 plus .25 x 100 (or $25) = $175

If the towns were 600 miles apart, however, National Movers would be cheaper. The cost of renting from National would be $275 compared to the $280 charged by Joe's Trucking.

Joe's - $100 plus .30 x 600 (or $180) = $280
National - $150 plus .25 x 500 (or $125) = $275

34. The answer is B. We've varied the format once more, but the reasoning is similar. This is a tedious question that is more like a math question, but we wanted to give you some practice with this type, just in case. You won't be able to do this question if you've forgotten how to do percents. Many exams require this knowledge, so if you feel you need a review we suggest you read Booklets 1, 2 or 3 in this series.

The only way to attack this problem is to go through each choice until you find the one that is correct. Choice A states that Plainfield, Smallville, and Granton are cities. Let's begin with Plainfield. The passage states that in 1990 Plainfield had a population of 12,000, and that it grew 10% between 1990 and 2000, and another 20% between 2000 and 2010. Ten percent of 12,000 is 1200 (12,000 x .10 = 1200). Therefore, the population grew from 12,000 in 1990 to 12,000 + 1200 between 1990 and 2000. At the time of the 2000 Census, Plainfield's population was 13,200. It then grew another 20% between 2000 and 2010, so, 13,200 x .20 = 2640. 13,200 plus the additional increase of 2640 would make the population of Plainfield 15,840. This would qualify it as a city, since its population is over 15,000. Since a change upward in the population of a municipality is re-classified immediately, Plainfield would have become a city right away. So far, statement A is true. The passage states that Smallville's population has not changed significantly in the last twenty years. Since Smallville's population was 20,283, Smallville would still be a city. Granton had a population of 25,000 (what a coincidence that so any of these places have such nice, even numbers) in 1980. The population has decreased 25% in each ten year period since that time. So from 1980 to 1990, the population decreased 25%. 25,000 x .25 = 6,250. 25,000 minus 6,250 = 18,750. So the population of Granton in 1990 would have been 18,750. (Or, you could have saved a step and multiplied 25,000 by .75 to get 18,750.) The population from 1990 to 2000 decreased an additional 25%. So: 18,750 x .25 = 4,687.50. 18,750 minus 4,687.50 = 14,062.50. Or: 18,750 x .75 = 14,062.50. (Don't let the fact that a half of a person is involved confuse you; these are exam questions, not real life.) From 2000 to 2010 the population decreased an additional 25%. This would mean that Granton's population was below 15,000 for more than ten years, so it's status as a city would have changed to that of a town, which would make choice A incorrect.

Choice B states that Smallville is a city and Granton is a town, which we know to be true from the information above. Choice B is correct so far. We next need to determine if Ellenville is a village. Ellenville had a population of 4,283 in 1980, and increased 5% in each ten year period since 1980. 4,283 x .05 = 214.15. 4,283 plus 214.15 = 4,497.15, so Ellenville's population from 1980 to 1990 increased to 4,497.15. (Or: 4,283 x 1.05 – 4,497.15.) From 1990 to 2000 Ellenville's population increased another 5%: 4,497.15 x .05 = 224.86. 4,497.15 plus 224.86 = 4,772.01 (or: 4,497.15 x 1.05 = 4,722.01.) From 2000 to 2010, Ellenville's population increased another 5%: 4,722.01 x .05 = 236.10. 4,722.01 plus 236.10 = 4,958.11. (Or: 4,722.01 x 1.05 = 4,958.11.).

Ellenville's population is still under 5,000 in 2010, so it would continue to be classified as a village. Since all three statements in choice B are true, choice B must be the answer. However, we'll go through the other choices. Choice C states that Springdale is a town. The passage tells us that the population of Springdale doubled from 1990 to 2000, and increased 25% from 2000 to 2010. It doesn't give us any actual population figures, however, so it's impossible to know what the population of Springdale is, making choice C incorrect. Choice C also states that Granton is a town, which is true, and that Ellenville is a town, which is false (from choice B we know it's a village). Choice D states that Plainfield and Smallville are cities, which is information we already know is true, and that Ellenville is a town. Since Ellenville is a village, choice D is also incorrect.

This was a lot of work for just one question and we doubt you'll get one like this on this section of the exam, but we included it just in case. On an exam, you can always put a check mark next to a question like this and come back to it later, if you feel you're pressed for time and cold spend your time more productively on other, less time-consuming problems.

35. The answer is B. This question requires very careful reading. It's best to break the conclusion down into smaller parts in order to solve the problem. The first half of the conclusion states that the average person in the 20-29 age group (Group A) drinks less tea daily than the average person in the 40-50 age group (Group C). The average person in Group A drinks 2.1 cups of tea daily, while the average person in Group C drinks 2.6 cups of tea daily. Since 2.1 is less than 2.6, the conclusion is correct so far. The second half of the conclusion states that the average person in Group A drinks more coffee daily than the average person in the 30-39 age group (Group B) drinks cola. The average person in Group A drinks 1.8 cups of coffee daily, while the average person in Group B drinks 1.9 glasses of cola. This disproves the conclusion, which states that the average person in Group A drinks more coffee daily than the average person in Group B drinks cola.

36. The answer is C. The easiest way to approach a problem that deals with the relationship between a number of different people or things is to set up a diagram. This type of problem is usually too confusing to do in your head. For this particular problem, the "diagram" could be a line, one end of which would be labeled tall and the other end labeled short. Then, taking one sentence at a time, place the people on the line to see where they fall in relation to one another.

The diagram of the first sentence would look like this:

Mary is taller than Jane but shorter than Dale, so she would fall somewhere between the two of them. We have placed tall on the left and labeled it left just to make the explanation easier. You could just as easily have reversed the position.

The second sentence places Fred somewhere to the left of Mary because he is taller than she is. Steven would be to the left of Fred for the same reason. At this point we don't know whether Steven and Fred are taller or shorter than Dale. The new diagram would look like this:

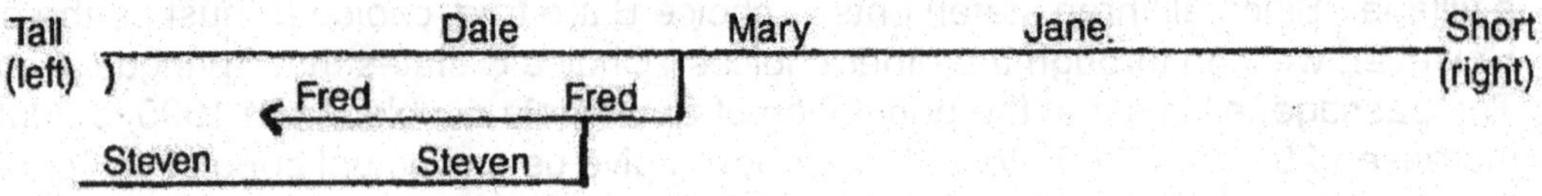

17 (#1)

The third sentence introduces Elizabeth, presenting a new problem. Elizabeth can be anywhere to the right of Dale. Don't make the mistake of assuming she falls between Dale and Mary. At this point we don't know where she fits in relation to Mary, Jane, or even Fred.

We do get information about Steven, however. He is taller than Dale so he would be to the left of Dale. Since he is also taller than Fred (see sentence II), we know that Steven is the tallest person thus far. The diagram would now look like this:

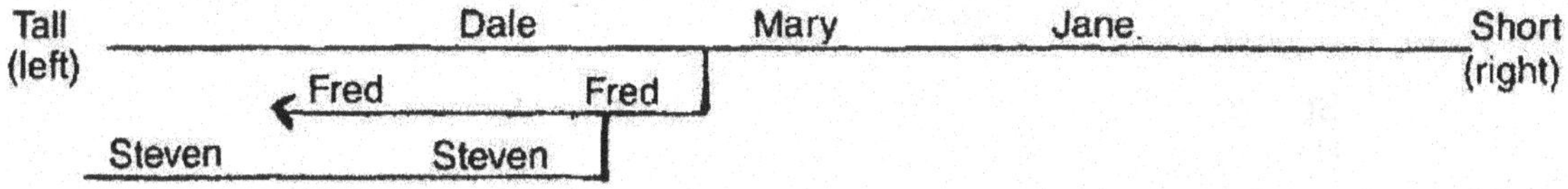

Fred's height is somewhere between Steven and Mary, Elizabeth's anywhere between Dale and the end of the line.

The fourth sentence tells us where Elizabeth stands, in relation to Fred and the others in the problem. The fact that she is taller than Mary means she is also taller than Jane. The final diagram would look like this:

We still don't know whether Dale or Fred is taller, however. Therefore, the conclusion that Dale is taller than Fred can't be proved. It also can't be disproved because we don't know for sure that he isn't. The answer has to be choice C, as the conclusion can't be proved or disproved.

37. The answer is A. This is another problem that is easiest for most people if they make a diagram. Sentence I states that Main Street is between Spring Street and Glenn Blvd. At this point we don't know if they are next to each other or if they are separated by a number of streets. Therefore, you should leave space between streets as you plot your first diagram.

The order of the streets could go either:

Spring St.	or	Glenn Blvd.
Main St.		Main St.
Glenn Blvd.		Spring St.

Sentence II states that Hawley Street is one block south of Spring Street and 3 blocks north of Main Street. Because most people think in terms of north as above and south as below and because it was stated that Hawley is one block south of Spring Street and three blocks north of Main Street, the next diagram could look like this:

Spring
Hawley
______
______
Main
Glenn

The third sentence states that Glenn Street is five blocks south of Elm and four blocks south of Main. It could look like this:

Spring
Hawley
______
Elm
Main
______
______
______
Glenn

The conclusion states that Elm Street is between Hawley Avenue and Glenn Blvd. From the above diagram, we can see that this is the case.

38. The answer is B. For most people, the best way to do this problem is to draw a diagram, plotting the course of both trains. Sentence I states that Train A leaves Hampshire at 5:50 A.M. and reaches New London at 6:42. Your first diagram might look like this:

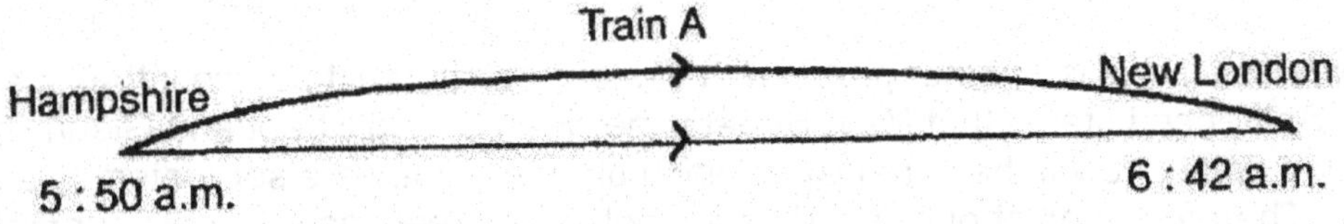

Sentence II states that the train leaves New London at 7:00 a.m. and arrives in Kellogsville at 8:42 a.m. The diagram might now look like this:

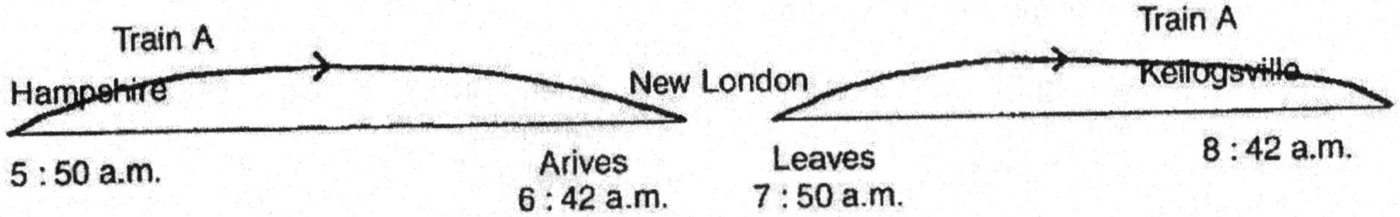

Sentence III gives us the rest of the information that must be included in the diagram. It introduces Train B, which moves in the opposite direction, leaving Kellogsville at 8:00 a.m. and arriving at Hampshire at 10:42 a.m. The final diagram might look like this:

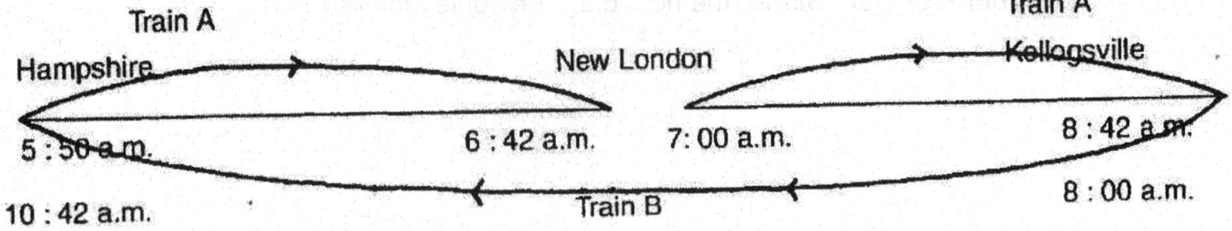

As you can see from the diagram, the routes of the two trains will overlap somewhere between Kellogsville and New London. If you read sentence IV quickly and assumed that that was the section with only one track, you probably would have assumed that there would have had to be a collision. Sentence IV states, however, that there is only one railroad track between New London and Hampshire. That is the only section, then, where the two trains could collide. By the time Train B gets to that section, however, Train A will have passed it. The two trains will pass each other somewhere between New London and Kellogsville, not New London and Hampshire.

EVALUATING CONCLUSIONS IN LIGHT OF KNOWN FACTS

EXAMINATION SECTION

TEST 1

DIRECTIONS: Each question or incomplete statement is followed by several suggested answers or completions. Select the one that BEST answers the question or completes the statement. *PRINT THE LETTER OF THE CORRECT ANSWER IN THE SPACE AT THE RIGHT.*

Questions 1-9.

DIRECTIONS: In Questions 1 through 9, you will read a set of facts and a conclusion drawn from them. The conclusion may be valid or invalid, based on the facts. It is your task to determine the validity of the conclusion.
For each question, select the letter before the statement that BEST expresses the relationship between the given facts and the conclusion that has been drawn from them. Your choices are:

A. The facts prove the conclusion.
B. The facts disprove the conclusion; or
C. The facts neither prove nor disprove the conclusion.

1. FACTS: Lauren must use Highway 29 to get to work. Lauren has a meeting today at 9:00 A.M. If she misses the meeting, Lauren will probably lose a major account. Highway 29 is closed all day today for repairs. 1.____

CONCLUSION: Lauren will not be able to get to work.

A. The facts prove the conclusion.
B. The facts disprove the conclusion.
C. The facts neither prove nor disprove the conclusion.

2. FACTS: The Tumbleweed Follies, a traveling burlesque show, is looking for a new line dancer. The position requires both singing and dancing skills. If the show cannot fill the position by Friday, it will begin to look for a magician to fill the time slot currently held by the line dancers. Willa, who wants to audition for the line dancing position, can sing, but cannot dance. 2.____

CONCLUSION: Willa is qualified to audition for the part of line dancer.

A. The facts prove the conclusion.
B. The facts disprove the conclusion.
C. The facts neither prove nor disprove the conclusion.

3. FACTS: Terry owns two dogs, Spike and Stan. One of the dogs is short-haired and has blue eyes. One dog as a pink nose. The blue-eyed dog never barks. One of the dogs has white fur on its paws. Sam has long hair. 3.____

CONCLUSION: Spike never barks.

A. The facts prove the conclusion.
B. The facts disprove the conclusion.
C. The facts neither prove nor disprove the conclusion.

4. FACTS: No science teachers are members of the PTA. Some English teachers are members of the PTA. Some English teachers in the PTA also wear glasses. Every PTA member is required to sit on the dunking stool at the student carnival except for those who wear glasses, who will be exempt. Those who are exempt, however, will have to officiate the hamster races. All of the English teachers in the PTA who do not wear glasses are married. 4.____

CONCLUSION: All the married English teachers in the PTA will set on the dunking stool at the student carnival.

A. The facts prove the conclusion.
B. The facts disprove the conclusion.
C. The facts neither prove nor disprove the conclusion.

5. FACTS: If the price of fuel is increased and sales remain constant, oil company profits will increase. The price of fuel was increased, and market experts project that sales levels are likely to be maintained. 5.____

CONCLUSION: The price of fuel will increase.

A. The facts prove the conclusion.
B. The facts disprove the conclusion.
C. The facts neither prove nor disprove the conclusion.

6. FACTS: Some members of the gymnastics team are double-jointed, and some members of the gymnastics team ae also on the lacrosse team. Some double-jointed members of the gymnastics team are also coaches. All gymnastics team members perform floor exercises, except the coaches. All the double-jointed members of the gymnastics team who are not coaches are freshmen. 6.____

CONCLUSION: Some double-jointed freshmen are coaches.

A. The facts prove the conclusion.
B. The facts disprove the conclusion.
C. The facts neither prove nor disprove the conclusion.

7. FACTS: Each member of the International Society speaks at least one foreign language, but no member speaks more than four foreign languages. Five members speak Spanish; three speak Mandarin; four speak French; four speak German; and five speak a foreign language other than Spanish, Mandarin, French, or German. 7.____

CONCLUSION: The lowest possible number of members in the International Society is eight.

A. The facts prove the conclusion.
B. The facts disprove the conclusion.
C. The facts neither prove nor disprove the conclusion.

8. FACTS: Mary keeps seven cats in her apartment. Only three of the cats will eat the same kind of food. Mary wants to keep at least one extra bag of each kind of food. 8.____

CONCLUSION: The minimum number of bags Mary will need to keep as extra is 7.

A. The facts prove the conclusion.
B. The facts disprove the conclusion.
C. The facts neither prove nor disprove the conclusion.

9. FACTS: In Ed and Marie's exercise group, everyone likes the treadmill or the stationary bicycle, or both, but Ed does not like the stationary bicycle. Marie has not expressed a preference, but spends most of her time on the stationary bicycle. 9.____

CONCLUSION: Everyone in the group who does not like the treadmill likes the stationary bicycle.

A. The facts prove the conclusion.
B. The facts disprove the conclusion.
C. The facts neither prove nor disprove the conclusion.

Questions 10-17.

DIRECTIONS: Questions 10 through 17 are based on the following reading passage. It is not your knowledge of the particular topic that is being tested, but your ability to reason based on what you have read. The passage is likely to detail several proposed courses of action and factors affecting these proposals. The reading passage is followed by a conclusion or outcome based on the facts in the passage, or a description of a decision taken regarding the situation. The conclusion is followed by a number of statements that have a possible connection to the conclusion. For each statement, you are to determine whether:

A. The statement proves the conclusion.
B. The statement supports the conclusion but does not prove it.
C. The statement disproves the conclusion.
D. The statement weakens the conclusion but does not disprove it.
E. The statement has no relevance to the conclusion.

Remember that the conclusion after the passage is to be accepted as the outcome of what actually happened, and that you are being asked to evaluate the impact each statement would have had on the conclusion.

PASSAGE

The Owyhee Mission School District's Board of Directors is hosting a public meeting to debate the merits of the proposed abolition of all bilingual education programs within the district. The group that has made the proposal believes the programs, which teach immigrant children academic subjects in their native language until they have learned English well enough to join mainstream classes, inhibit the ability of students to acquire English quickly and succeed in school and in the larger American society. Such programs, they argue, are also a wasteful drain on the district's already scant resources.

At the meeting, several teachers and parents stand to speak out against the proposal. The purpose of an education, they say, should be to build upon, rather than dismantle, a minority child's language and culture. By teaching children in academic subjects in their native tongues, while simultaneously offering English language instruction, schools can meet the goals of learning English and progressing through academic subjects along with their peers.

Hiram Nguyen, a representative of the parents whose children are currently enrolled in bilingual education, stands at the meeting to express the parents' wishes. The parents have been polled, he says, and are overwhelmingly of the opinion that while language and culture are important to them, they are not things that will disappear from the students' lives if they are no longer taught in the classroom. The most important issue for the parents is whether their children will succeed in school and be competitive in the larger American society. If bilingual education can be demonstrated to do that, then the parents are in favor of continuing it.

At the end of the meeting, a proponent of the plan, Oscar Ramos, stands to clarify some misconceptions about the proposal. It does not call for a "sink or swim" approach, he says, but allows for an interpreter to be present in mainstream classes to explain anything a student finds too complex or confusing.

The last word of the meeting is given to Delia Cruz, a bilingual teacher at one of the district's elementary schools. A student is bound to find anything complex or confusing, she says, if it is spoken in a language he has never heard before. It is more wasteful to place children in classrooms where they don't understand anything, she says, than it is to try to teach them something useful as they are learning the English language.

CONCLUSION: After the meeting, the Owyhee Mission School District's Board of Directors votes to terminate all the district's bilingual education programs at the end of the current academic year, but to maintain the current level of funding to each of the schools that have programs cut.

10. A poll conducted by the *Los Angeles Times* at approximately the same time as the Board's meeting indicated that 75% of the people were opposed to bilingual education; among Latinos, opposition was 84%. 10.____
   A. The statement proves the conclusion.
   B. The statement supports the conclusion but does not prove it.
   C. The statement disproves the conclusion.
   D. The statement weakens the conclusion but does not disprove it.
   E. The statement has no relevance to the conclusion.

11. Of all the studies connected on bilingual education programs, 64% indicate that students learned English grammar better in "sink or swim" classes without any special features than they did in bilingual education classes. 11.____
   A. The statement proves the conclusion.
   B. The statement supports the conclusion but does not prove it.
   C. The statement disproves the conclusion.
   D. The statement weakens the conclusion but does not disprove it.
   E. The statement has no relevance to the conclusion.

12. In the academic year that begins after the Board's vote, Montgomery Burns Elementary, an Owyhee Mission District school, launches a new bilingual program for the children of Somali immigrants. 12.____
   A. The statement proves the conclusion.
   B. The statement supports the conclusion but does not prove it.
   C. The statement disproves the conclusion.
   D. The statement weakens the conclusion but does not disprove it.
   E. The statement has no relevance to the conclusion.

13. In the previous academic year, under severe budget restraints, the Owyhee Mission District cut all physical education, music, and art classes, but its funding for bilingual education classes increased by 18%. 13.____
   A. The statement proves the conclusion.
   B. The statement supports the conclusion but does not prove it.
   C. The statement disproves the conclusion.
   D. The statement weakens the conclusion but does not disprove it.
   E. The statement has no relevance to the conclusion.

14. Before the Board votes, a polling consultant conducts randomly sampled assessments of immigrant students who enrolled in Owyhee District schools at a time when they did not speak any English at all. Ten years after graduating from high school, 44% of those who received bilingual education were professionals – doctors, lawyers, educators, engineers, etc. Of those who did not receive bilingual education, 38% were professionals. 14.____
   A. The statement proves the conclusion.
   B. The statement supports the conclusion but does not prove it.
   C. The statement disproves the conclusion.
   D. The statement weakens the conclusion but does not disprove it.
   E. The statement has no relevance to the conclusion.

15. Over the past several years, the scores of Owyhee District students have gradually declined, and enrollment numbers have followed as anxious parents transferred their children to other schools or applied for a state-funded voucher program. 15.____
   A. The statement proves the conclusion.
   B. The statement supports the conclusion but does not prove it.
   C. The statement disproves the conclusion.
   D. The statement weakens the conclusion but does not disprove it.
   E. The statement has no relevance to the conclusion.

16. California and Massachusetts, two of the most liberal states in the country, have each passed ballot measures banning bilingual education in public schools. 16.____
   A. The statement proves the conclusion.
   B. The statement supports the conclusion but does not prove it.
   C. The statement disproves the conclusion.
   D. The statement weakens the conclusion but does not disprove it.
   E. The statement has no relevance to the conclusion.

17. In the academic year that begins after the Board's vote, no Owyhee Mission Schools are conducting bilingual instruction. 17.____
   A. The statement proves the conclusion.
   B. The statement supports the conclusion but does not prove it.
   C. The statement disproves the conclusion.
   D. The statement weakens the conclusion but does not disprove it.
   E. The statement has no relevance to the conclusion.

Questions 18-25.

DIRECTIONS: Questions 18 through 25 each provide four factual statements and a conclusion based on these statements. After reading the entire question, you will decide whether:
   A. The conclusion is proved by Statements 1-4;
   B. The conclusion is disproved by Statements 1-4;
   C. The facts are not sufficient to prove or disprove the conclusion.

18. FACTUAL STATEMENTS: 18.____
   1) Gear X rotates in a clockwise direction if Switch C is in the OFF position.
   2) Gear X will rotate in a counter-clockwise direction if Switch C is ON.
   3) If Gear X is rotating in a clockwise direction, then Gear Y will not be rotating at all.
   4) Switch C is OFF.

   CONCLUSION: Gear Y is rotating.

   A. The conclusion is proved by Statements 1-4;
   B. The conclusion is disproved by Statements 1-4;
   C. The facts are not sufficient to prove or disprove the conclusion.

19. FACTUAL STATEMENTS: 19.____
1) Mark is older than Jim but younger than Dan.
2) Fern is older than Mark but younger than Silas.
3) Dan is younger than Silas but older than Edward.
4) Edward is older than Mark but younger than Fern.

CONCLUSION: Dan is older than Fern.

A. The conclusion is proved by Statements 1-4;
B. The conclusion is disproved by Statements 1-4;
C. The facts are not sufficient to prove or disprove the conclusion.

20. FACTUAL STATEMENTS: 20.____
1) Each of Fred's three sofa cushions lies on top of four lost coins.
2) The cushion on the right covers two pennies and two dimes.
3) The middle cushion covers two dimes and two quarters.
4) The cushion on the left covers two nickels and two quarters.

CONCLUSION: To be guaranteed of retrieving at least one coin of each denomination, and without looking at any of the coins, Frank must take three coins each from under the cushions on the right and the left.

A. The conclusion is proved by Statements 1-4;
B. The conclusion is disproved by Statements 1-4;
C. The facts are not sufficient to prove or disprove the conclusion.

21. FACTUAL STATEMENTS: 21.____
1) The door to the hammer mill chamber is locked if light 6 is red.
2) The door to the hammer mill chamber is locked only when the mill is operating.
3) If the mill is not operating, light 6 is blue.
4) The door to the hammer mill chamber is locked.

CONCLUSION: The mill is in operation.

A. The conclusion is proved by Statements 1-4;
B. The conclusion is disproved by Statements 1-4;
C. The facts are not sufficient to prove or disprove the conclusion.

22. FACTUAL STATEMENTS: 22.____
1) In a five-story office building, where each story is occupied by a single professional, Dr. Kane's office is above Dr. Assad's.
2) Dr. Johnson's office is between Dr. Kane's and Dr. Conlon's.
3) Dr. Steen's office is between Dr. Conlon's and Dr. Assad's.
4) Dr. Johnson is on the fourth story.

CONCLUSION: Dr. Steen occupies the second story.

A. The conclusion is proved by Statements 1-4;
B. The conclusion is disproved by Statements 1-4;
C. The facts are not sufficient to prove or disprove the conclusion.

23. FACTUAL STATEMENTS: 23.____

1) On Saturday, farmers Hank, Earl, Roy, and Cletus plowed a total of 520 acres.
2) Hank plowed twice as many acres as Roy.
3) Roy plowed half as much as the farmer who plowed the most.
4) Cletus plowed 160 acres.

CONCLUSION: Hank plowed 200 acres.

A. The conclusion is proved by Statements 1-4;
B. The conclusion is disproved by Statements 1-4;
C. The facts are not sufficient to prove or disprove the conclusion.

24. FACTUAL STATEMENTS: 24.____

1) Four travelers – Tina, Jodie, Alex, and Oscar – each traveled to a different island – Aruba, Jamaica, Nevis, and Barbados – but not necessarily respectively.
2) Tina did not travel as far to Jamaica as Jodie traveled to her island.
3) Oscar traveled twice as far as Alex, who traveled the same distance as the traveler who went to Aruba.
4) Oscar went to Barbados.

CONCLUSION: Oscar traveled the farthest.

A. The conclusion is proved by Statements 1-4;
B. The conclusion is disproved by Statements 1-4;
C. The facts are not sufficient to prove or disprove the conclusion.

25. FACTUAL STATEMENT: 25.____

1) In the natural history museum, every Native American display that contains pottery also contains beadwork.
2) Some of the displays containing lodge replicas also contain beadwork.
3) The display on the Choctaw, a Native American tribe, contains pottery.
4) The display on the Modoc, a Native American tribe, contains only two of these items.

CONCLUSION: If the Modoc display contains pottery, it does not contain lodge replicas.

A. The conclusion is proved by Statements 1-4;
B. The conclusion is disproved by Statements 1-4;
C. The facts are not sufficient to prove or disprove the conclusion.

KEY (CORRECT ANSWERS)

1. A
2. B
3. A
4. A
5. C

6. B
7. B
8. B
9. A
10. B

11. B
12. C
13. B
14. D
15. E

16. E
17. A
18. B
19. C
20. A

21. A
22. A
23. C
24. A
25. A

TEST 2

DIRECTIONS: Each question or incomplete statement is followed by several suggested answers or completions. Select the one that BEST answers the question or completes the statement. *PRINT THE LETTER OF THE CORRECT ANSWER IN THE SPACE AT THE RIGHT.*

Questions 1-9.

DIRECTIONS: In Questions 1 through 9, you will read a set of facts and a conclusion drawn from them. The conclusion may be valid or invalid, based on the facts. It is your task to determine the validity of the conclusion.
For each question, select the letter before the statement that BEST expresses the relationship between the given facts and the conclusion that has been drawn from them. Your choices are:

A. The facts prove the conclusion.
B. The facts disprove the conclusion; or
C. The facts neither prove nor disprove the conclusion.

1. FACTS: If the maximum allowable income for Medicaid recipients is increased, the number of Medicaid recipients will increase. If the number of Medicaid recipients increases, more funds must be allocated to the Medicaid program, which will require a tax increase. Taxes cannot be approved without the approval of the legislature. The legislature probably will not approve a tax increase. 1.____

CONCLUSION: The maximum allowable income for Medicaid recipients will increase.

A. The facts prove the conclusion.
B. The facts disprove the conclusion; or
C. The facts neither prove nor disprove the conclusion.

2. FACTS: All the dentists on the baseball team are short. Everyone in the dugout is a dentist, but not everyone in the dugout is short. The baseball team is not made up of people of any particular profession. 2.____

CONCLUSION: Some people who are not dentists are in the dugout.

A. The facts prove the conclusion.
B. The facts disprove the conclusion; or
C. The facts neither prove nor disprove the conclusion.

3. FACTS: A taxi company's fleet is divided into two fleets. Fleet One contains cabs A, B, C, and D. Fleet Two contains E, F, G, and H. Each cab is either yellow or green. Five of the cabs are yellow. Cabs A and E are not both yellow. Either Cab C or F, or both, are not yellow. Cabs B and H are either both yellow or both green. 3.____

CONCLUSION: Cab H is green.

A. The facts prove the conclusion.
B. The facts disprove the conclusion; or
C. The facts neither prove nor disprove the conclusion.

4. FACTS: Most people in the skydiving club are not afraid of heights. Everyone in the skydiving club makes three parachute jumps a month. 4.____

CONCLUSION: At least one person who is afraid of heights makes three parachute jumps a month.

A. The facts prove the conclusion.
B. The facts disprove the conclusion; or
C. The facts neither prove nor disprove the conclusion.

5. FACTS: If the Board approves the new rule, the agency will move to a new location immediately. If the agency moves, five new supervisors will be immediately appointed. The Board has approved the new proposal. 5.____

CONCLUSION: No new supervisors were appointed.

A. The facts prove the conclusion.
B. The facts disprove the conclusion; or
C. The facts neither prove nor disprove the conclusion.

6. FACTS: All the workers at the supermarket chew gum when they sack groceries. Sometimes Lance, a supermarket worker, doesn't chew gum at all when he works. Another supermarket worker, Jenny, chews gum the whole time she is at work. 6.____

CONCLUSION: Jenny always sacks groceries when she is at work.

7. FACTS: Lake Lottawatta is bigger than Lake Tacomi. Lake Tacomi and Lake Ottawa are exactly the same size. All lakes in Montana are bigger than Lake Ottawa. 7.____

CONCLUSION: Lake Lottawatta is in Montana.

A. The facts prove the conclusion.
B. The facts disprove the conclusion; or
C. The facts neither prove nor disprove the conclusion.

8. FACTS: Two men, Cox and Taylor, are playing poker at a table. Taylor has a pair of aces in his hand. One man is smoking a cigar. One of them has no pairs in his hand and is wearing an eye patch. The man wearing the eye patch is smoking a cigar. One man is bald. 8.____

CONCLUSION: Cox is smoking a cigar.

A. The facts prove the conclusion.
B. The facts disprove the conclusion; or
C. The facts neither prove nor disprove the conclusion.

9. FACTS: All Kwakiutls are Wakashan Indians. All Wakashan Indians originated on Vancouver Island. The Nootka also originated on Vancouver Island. 9.____

CONCLUSION: Kwakiutls originated on Vancouver Island.

A. The facts prove the conclusion.
B. The facts disprove the conclusion; or
C. The facts neither prove nor disprove the conclusion.

Questions 10-17.

DIRECTIONS: Questions 10 through 17 are based on the following reading passage. It is not your knowledge of the particular topic that is being tested, but your ability to reason based on what you have read. The passage is likely to detail several proposed courses of action and factors affecting these proposals. The reading passage is followed by a conclusion or outcome based on the facts in the passage, or a description of a decision taken regarding the situation. The conclusion is followed by a number of statements that have a possible connection to the conclusion. For each statement, you are to determine whether:

A. The statement proves the conclusion.
B. The statement supports the conclusion but does not prove it.
C. The statement disproves the conclusion.
D. The statement weakens the conclusion but does not disprove it.
E. The statement has no relevance to the conclusion.

Remember that the conclusion after the passage is to be accepted as the outcome of what actually happened, and that you are being asked to evaluate the impact each statement would have had on the conclusion.

PASSAGE

The World Wide Web portal and search engine, HipBot, is considering becoming a subscription-only service, locking out nonsubscribers from the content on its web site. HipBot currently relies solely on advertising revenues.

HipBot's content director says that by taking in an annual fee from each customer, the company can both increase profits and provide premium content that no other portal can match.

The marketing director disagrees, saying that there is no guarantee that anyone who now visits the web site for free will agree to pay for the privilege of visiting it again. Most will probably simply use the other major portals. Also, HipBot's advertising clients will not be happy when they learn that the site will be viewed by a more limited number of people.

CONCLUSION: In January of 2016, the CEO of HipBot decides to keep the portal open to all web users, with some limited "premium content" available to subscribers who don't mind paying a little extra to access it. The company will aim to maintain, or perhaps increase, its advertising revenue.

10. In an independent marketing survey, 62% of respondents said they "strongly agree" with the following statement: "I almost never pay attention to advertisements that appear on the World Wide Web." 10.____
    A. The statement proves the conclusion.
    B. The statement supports the conclusion but does not prove it.
    C. The statement disproves the conclusion.
    D. The statement weakens the conclusion but does not disprove it.
    E. The statement has no relevance to the conclusion.

11. When it learns about the subscription-only debate going on at HipBot, Wernham Hogg Entertainment, one of HipBot's most reliable clients, says it will withdraw its ads and place them on a free web portal if HipBot decides to limit its content to subscribers. Wernham Hogg pays HipBot about $6 million annually – about 12% of HipBot's gross revenues – to run its ads online. 11.____
    A. The statement proves the conclusion.
    B. The statement supports the conclusion but does not prove it.
    C. The statement disproves the conclusion.
    D. The statement weakens the conclusion but does not disprove it.
    E. The statement has no relevance to the conclusion.

12. At the end of the second quarter of FY 2016, after continued stagnant profits, the CEO of HipBot assembles a blue ribbon commission to gather and analyze data on the costs, benefits, and feasibility of adding a limited amount of "premium" content to the HipBot portal. 12.____
    A. The statement proves the conclusion.
    B. The statement supports the conclusion but does not prove it.
    C. The statement disproves the conclusion.
    D. The statement weakens the conclusion but does not disprove it.
    E. The statement has no relevance to the conclusion.

13. In the following fiscal year, Wernham Hogg Entertainment, satisfied with the "hit counts" on HipBot's free web site, spends another $1 million on advertisements that will appear on web pages that are available to HipBot's "premium subscribers. 13.____
    A. The statement proves the conclusion.
    B. The statement supports the conclusion but does not prove it.
    C. The statement disproves the conclusion.
    D. The statement weakens the conclusion but does not disprove it.
    E. The statement has no relevance to the conclusion.

14. HipBot's information technology director reports that the engineers in his department have come up with a feature that will search not only individual web pages, but tie into other web-based search engines, as well, and then comb through all these results to find those most relevant to the user's search. 14.____

A. The statement proves the conclusion.
B. The statement supports the conclusion but does not prove it.
C. The statement disproves the conclusion.
D. The statement weakens the conclusion but does not disprove it.
E. The statement has no relevance to the conclusion.

15. In an independent marketing survey, 79% of respondents said they "strongly agree" with the following statement: "Many web sites are so dominated by advertisements these days that it is increasingly frustrating to find the content I want to read or see." 15.____
A. The statement proves the conclusion.
B. The statement supports the conclusion but does not prove it.
C. The statement disproves the conclusion.
D. The statement weakens the conclusion but does not disprove it.
E. The statement has no relevance to the conclusion.

16. After three years of studies at the federal level, the Department of Commerce releases a report suggesting that, in general, the only private "subscriber-only" web sites that do well financially are those with a very specialized user population. 16.____
A. The statement proves the conclusion.
B. The statement supports the conclusion but does not prove it.
C. The statement disproves the conclusion.
D. The statement weakens the conclusion but does not disprove it.
E. The statement has no relevance to the conclusion.

17. HipBot's own marketing research indicates that the introduction of premium content has the potential to attract new users to the HipBot portal. 17.____
A. The statement proves the conclusion.
B. The statement supports the conclusion but does not prove it.
C. The statement disproves the conclusion.
D. The statement weakens the conclusion but does not disprove it.
E. The statement has no relevance to the conclusion.

Questions 18-25.

DIRECTIONS: Questions 18 through 25 each provide four factual statements and a conclusion based on these statements. After reading the entire question, you will decide whether:
A. The conclusion is proved by Statements 1-4;
B. The conclusion is disproved by Statements 1-4;
C. The facts are not sufficient to prove or disprove the conclusion.

18. FACTUAL STATEMENTS: 18.____
    1) If the alarm goes off, Sam will wake up.
    2) If Tandy wakes up before 4:00, Linda will leave the bedroom and sleep on the couch.
    3) If Linda leaves the bedroom, she'll check the alarm to make sure it is working.
    4) The alarm goes off.

    CONCLUSION: Tandy woke up before 4:00.

    A. The conclusion is proved by Statements 1-4;
    B. The conclusion is disproved by Statements 1-4;
    C. The facts are not sufficient to prove or disprove the conclusion.

19. FACTUAL STATEMENTS: 19.____
    1) Four brothers are named Earl, John, Gary, and Pete.
    2) Earl and Pete are unmarried.
    3) John is shorter than the youngest of the four.
    4) The oldest brother is married, and is also the tallest.

    CONCLUSION: Pete is the youngest brother.

    A. The conclusion is proved by Statements 1-4;
    B. The conclusion is disproved by Statements 1-4;
    C. The facts are not sufficient to prove or disprove the conclusion.

20. FACTUAL STATEMENTS: 20.____
    1) Automobile engines are cooled either by air or by liquid.
    2) If the engine is small and simple enough, air from a belt-driven fan will cool it sufficiently.
    3) Most newer automobile engines are too complicated to be air-cooled.
    4) Air-cooled engines are cheaper and easier to build then liquid-cooled engines.

    CONCLUSION: Most newer automobile engines use liquid coolant.

    A. The conclusion is proved by Statements 1-4;
    B. The conclusion is disproved by Statements 1-4;
    C. The facts are not sufficient to prove or disprove the conclusion.

21. FACTUAL STATEMENTS: 21.____
    1) Erica will only file a lawsuit if she is injured while parasailing.
    2) If Rick orders Trip to run a rope test, Trip will check the rigging.
    3) If the rigging does not malfunction, Erica will not be injured.
    4) Rick orders Trip to run a rope test.

CONCLUSION: Erica does not file a lawsuit.

A. The conclusion is proved by Statements 1-4;
B. The conclusion is disproved by Statements 1-4;
C. The facts are not sufficient to prove or disprove the conclusion.

22. FACTUAL STATEMENTS: 22.____

1) On Maple Street, which is four blocks long, Bill's shop is two blocks east of Ken's shop.
2) Ken's shop is one block west of the only shop on Maple Street with an awning.
3) Erma's shop is one block west of the easternmost block.
4) Bill's shop is on the easternmost block.

CONCLUSION: Bill's shop has an awning.

A. The conclusion is proved by Statements 1-4;
B. The conclusion is disproved by Statements 1-4;
C. The facts are not sufficient to prove or disprove the conclusion.

23. FACTUAL STATEMENTS: 23.____

1) Gear X rotates in a clockwise direction if Switch C is in the OFF position.
2) Gear X will rotate in a counter-clockwise direction if Switch C is ON.
3) If Gear X is rotating in a clockwise direction, then Gear Y will not be rotating at all.
4) Gear Y is rotating.

CONCLUSION: Gear X is rotating in a counter-clockwise direction.

A. The conclusion is proved by Statements 1-4;
B. The conclusion is disproved by Statements 1-4;
C. The facts are not sufficient to prove or disprove the conclusion.

24. FACTUAL STATEMENTS: 24.____

1) The Republic of Garbanzo's currency system has four basic denominations: the pastor, the noble, the donner, and the rojo.
2) A pastor is worth 2 nobles.
3) 2 donners can be exchanged for a rojo.
4) 3 pastors are equal in value to 2 donners.

CONCLUSION: The rojo is most valuable.

A. The conclusion is proved by Statements 1-4;
B. The conclusion is disproved by Statements 1-4;
C. The facts are not sufficient to prove or disprove the conclusion.

25. FACTUAL STATEMENTS: 25.____
    1) At Prickett's Nursery, the only citrus trees left are either Meyer lemons or Valencia oranges, and every citrus tree left is either a dwarf or a semidwarf.
    2) Half of the semidwarf trees are Meyer lemons.
    3) There are more semidwarf trees left than dwarf trees.
    4) A quarter of the dwarf trees are Valencia oranges.

    CONCLUSION: There are more Valencia oranges left at Prickett's Nursery than Meyer lemons.

    A. The conclusion is proved by Statements 1-4;
    B. The conclusion is disproved by Statements 1-4;
    C. The facts are not sufficient to prove or disprove the conclusion.

KEY (CORRECT ANSWERS)

1. C
2. B
3. B
4. A
5. B

6. C
7. C
8. A
9. A
10. E

11. B
12. C
13. A
14. E
15. D

16. B
17. B
18. C
19. C
20. A

21. C
22. B
23. C
24. A
25. B

READING COMPREHENSION
UNDERSTANDING AND INTERPRETING WRITTEN MATERIAL

EXAMINATION SECTION

TEST 1

DIRECTIONS: Each question or incomplete statement is followed by several suggested answers or completions. Select the one that BEST answers the question or completes the statement. *PRINT THE LETTER OF THE CORRECT ANSWER IN THE SPACE AT THE RIGHT.*

Questions 1-4.

DIRECTIONS: Questions 1 through 4 are to be answered SOLELY on the basis of the following paragraph.

An annual leave allowance, which combines leaves previously given for vacation, personal business, family illness, and other reasons shall be granted members. Calculation of credits for such leave shall be on an annual basis beginning January 1st of each year. Annual leave credits shall be based on time served by members during preceding calendar year. However, when credits have been accrued and member retires during current year, additional annual leave credits shall, in this instance, be granted at accrual rate of three days for each completed month of service, excluding terminal leave. If accruals granted for completed months of service extend into following month, member shall be granted an additional three days accrual for completed month. This shall be the only condition where accruals in a current year are granted for vacation period in such year.

1. According to the above paragraph, if a fireman's wife were to become seriously ill so that he would take time off from work to be with her, such time off would be deducted from his _____ leave allowance. 1.____
   A. annual
   B. vacation
   C. personal business
   D. family illness

2. Terminal leave means leave taken 2.____
   A. at the end of the calendar year
   B. at the end of the vacation year
   C. immediately before retirement
   D. before actually earned, because of an emergency

3. A fireman appointed on July 1, 2017 will be able to take his first full or normal annual leave during the period 3.____
   A. July 1, 2017 to June 30, 2018
   B. Jan. 1, 2018 to Dec. 31, 2018
   C. July 1, 2018 to June 30, 2019
   D. Jan. 1, 2019 to Dec. 31, 2019

4. According to the above paragraph, a member who retires on July 15 of this year will be entitled to receive leave allowance based on this year of _____ days. 4.____
   A. 15
   B. 18
   C. 22
   D. 24

5. Fire alarm boxes are electromechanical devices for transmitting a coded signal. In each box, there is a trainwork of wheels. When the box is operated, a spring-activated code wheel begins to revolve. The code number of the box is etched on the circumference of the code wheel, and the latter is associated with the circuit in such a way that when it revolves it causes the circuit to open and close in a predetermined manner, thereby transmitting its particular signal to the central station. A fire alarm box is nothing more than a device for interrupting the flow of current in a circuit in such a way as to produce a coded signal that may be decoded by the dispatchers in the central office. 5.____
Based on the above, select the FALSE statement.
   A. Each standard fire alarm box has its own code wheel.
   B. The code wheel operates when the box is pulled.
   C. The code wheel is operated electrically.
   D. Only the break in the circuit by the notched wheel causes the alarm signal to be transmitted to the central office.

Questions 6-9.

DIRECTIONS: Questions 6 through 9 are to be answered SOLELY on the basis of the following paragraph.

Ventilation, as used in firefighting operations, means opening up a building or structure in which a fire is burning to release the accumulated heat, smoke, and gases. Lack of knowledge of the principles of ventilation on the part of firemen may result in unnecessary punishment due to ventilation being neglected or improperly handled. While ventilation itself extinguishes no fires, when used in an intelligent manner, it allows firemen to get at the fire more quickly, easily, and with less danger and hardship.

6. According to the above paragraph, the MOST important result of failure to apply the principles of ventilation at a fire may be 6.____
   A. loss of public confidence
   B. waste of water
   C. excessive use of equipment
   D. injury to firemen

7. It may be inferred from the above paragraph that the CHIEF advantage of ventilation is that it 7.____
   A. eliminates the need for gas masks
   B. reduces smoke damage
   C. permits firemen to work closer to the fire
   D. cools the fire

8. Knowledge of the principles of ventilation, as defined in the above paragraph, would be LEAST important in a fire in a 8.____
   A. tenement house
   B. grocery store
   C. ship's hold
   D. lumberyard

9. We may conclude from the above paragraph that for the well-trained and equipped fireman, ventilation is 9.____
   A. a simple matter
   B. rarely necessary
   C. relatively unimportant
   D. a basic tool

Questions 10-13.

DIRECTIONS: Questions 10 through 13 are to be answered SOLELY on the basis of the following passage.

Fire exit drills should be established and held periodically to effectively train personnel to leave their working area promptly upon proper signal and to evacuate the building, speedily but without confusion. All fire exit drills should be carefully planned and carried out in a serious manner under rigid discipline so as to provide positive protection in the event of a real emergency. As a general rule, the local fire department should be furnished advance information regarding the exact date and time the exit drill is scheduled. When it is impossible to hold regular drills, written instructions should be distributed to all employees.

Depending upon individual circumstances, fires in warehouses vary from those of fast development that are almost instantly beyond any possibility of employee control to others of relatively slow development where a small readily attackable flame may be present for periods of time up to 15 minutes or more during which simple attack with fire extinguishers or small building hoses may prevent the fire development. In any case, it is characteristic of many warehouse fires that at a certain point in development they flash up to the top of the stack, increase heat quickly, and spread rapidly. There is a degree of inherent danger in attacking warehouse type fires, and all employees should be thoroughly trained in the use of the types of extinguishers or small hoses in the buildings and well instructed in the necessity of always staying between the fire and a direct pass to an exit.

10. Employees should be instructed that, when fighting a fire, they MUST 10.____
    A. try to control the blaze
    B. extinguish any fire in 15 minutes
    C. remain between the fire and a direct passage to the exit
    D. keep the fire between themselves and the fire exit

11. Whenever conditions are such that regular fire drills cannot be held, then which one of the following actions should be taken? 11.____
    A. The local fire department should be notified.
    B. Rigid discipline should be maintained during work hours.
    C. Personnel should be instructed to leave their working area by whatever means are available.
    D. Employees should receive fire drill procedures in writing.

12. The above passage indicates that the purpose of fire exit drills is to train employees to 12.____
    A. control a fire before it becomes uncontrollable
    B. act as firefighters
    C. leave the working area promptly
    D. be serious

13. According to the above passage, fire exit drills will prove to be of UTMOST effectiveness if 13.____
   A. employee participation is made voluntary
   B. they take place periodically
   C. the fire department actively participates
   D. they are held without advance planning

Questions 14-16.

DIRECTIONS: Questions 14 through 16 are to be answered SOLELY on the basis of the following paragraph.

The heat output from unit heaters will depend on how fast and how completely dry hot steam fills the unit core. For complete and fast air removal and rapid drainage of condensate, use a trap actuated by water or vapor (inverted bucket trap) and not a trap operated by temperature only (thermostatic or bellows trap). A temperature-actuated trap will hold back the hot condensate until it cools to a point where the thermal element opens. When this happens, the condensate backs up in the heater and reduces the heat output. With a water-actuated trap, this will not happen as the water or condensate is discharged as fast as it is formed.

14. On the basis of the information given in the above paragraph, it can be concluded that the PROPER type of trap to use for a unit heater is a(n) _____ trap. 14.____
   A. thermostatic
   B bellows-type
   C. inverted bucket
   D. temperature

15. According to the above paragraph, the MAIN reason for using the type of trap specified for a unit heater is to 15.____
   A. bring the condensate up to steam temperature
   B. prevent reduction in the heat output of the unit heater
   C. permit cycling of the heater
   D. maintain constant temperature of condensate in the trap

16. As used in the above paragraph, the word *actuated* means MOST NEARLY 16.____
   A. clogged B. operated C. cleaned D. vented

Questions 17-25.

DIRECTIONS: Questions 17 through 25 are to be answered SOLELY on the basis of the following passage. Each question consists of a statement. You are to indicate whether the statement is TRUE (T) or FALSE (F).

<u>MOVING AN OFFICE</u>

An office with all its equipment is sometimes moved during working hours. This is a difficult task and must be done in an orderly manner to avoid confusion. The operation should be planned in such a way as not to interrupt the progress of work usually done in the office and to make possible the accurate placement of the furniture and records in the new location. If the office moves to a place inside the same building, the desks and files are moved with all their contents. If the movement is to another building, the contents of each desk and file are placed in boxes. Each box is marked with a letter showing the particular section in the new quarters to which it is to be moved. Also marked on each box is the number of the desk or file on which the box is to be placed. Each piece of equipment must have a numbered tag. The number of each piece of equipment is put in soft chalk on the floor in the new office to show the proper location, and several floor plans are made to show where each piece of equipment goes. When the moving is done, someone is stationed at each of the several exits of the old office to see that each box or piece of equipment has its destination clearly marked on it. At the new office, someone stands at each of the several entrances with a copy of the floor plan and directs the placing of the furniture and equipment according to the floor plan. No one should interfere at this point with the arrangements shown on the plan. Improvements in arrangement can be considered and made at a later date.

17. It is a hard job to move an office from one place to another during working hours. 17.____

18. Confusion cannot be avoided if an office is moved during working hours. 18.____

19. The work usually done in an office must be stopped for the day when the office is moved during working hours. 19.____

20. If an office is moved from one floor to another in the same building, the contents of a desk are taken out and put into boxes for moving. 20.____

21. If boxes are used to hold material from desks when moving an office, the box is numbered the same as the desk on which it is to be put. 21.____

22. Letters are marked in soft chalk on the floor at the new quarters to show where the desks should go when moved. 22.____

23. When the moving begins, a person is put at each exit of the old office to check that each box and piece of equipment has clearly marked on it where to go. 23.____

24. A person stationed at each entrance of the new quarters to direct the placing of the furniture and equipment has a copy of the floor plan of the new quarters. 24.____

25. If, while the furniture is being moved into the new office, a person helping at a doorway gets an idea of a better way to arrange the furniture, he should change the planned arrangement and make a record of the change. 25.____

KEY (CORRECT ANSWERS)

1. A
2. C
3. D
4. B
5. C

6. D
7. C
8. D
9. D
10. C

11. D
12. C
13. B
14. C
15. B

16. B
17. T
18. F
19. F
20. F

21. T
22. F
23. T
24. T
25. F

TEST 2

DIRECTIONS: Each question or incomplete statement is followed by several suggested answers or completions. Select the one that BEST answers the question or completes the statement. *PRINT THE LETTER OF THE CORRECT ANSWER IN THE SPACE AT THE RIGHT.*

Questions 1-4.

DIRECTIONS: Questions 1 through 4 are to be answered SOLELY on the basis of the following paragraph.

In all cases of homicide, members of the Police Department who investigate will make every effort to obtain statements from dying persons. Such statements are of the greatest importance to the District Attorney. In many cases, there may be a failure to solve the crime if they are not taken. The principal element to be considered in taking the declaration of a dying person is his mental attitude. In order to be admissible in evidence, the person must have no hope of recovery. The patient will be fully interrogated on that point before a statement is taken.

1. In cases of homicide, according to the above paragraph, members of the police force will 1.____
   A. try to change the mental attitude of the dying person
   B. attempt to obtain a statement from the dying person
   C. not give the information they obtain directly to the District Attorney
   D. be careful not to injure the dying person unnecessarily

2. The mental attitude of the person making the dying statement is of GREAT importance because it can determine, according to the above paragraph, whether the 2.____
   A. victim should be interrogated in the presence of witnesses
   B. victim will be willing to make a statement of any kind
   C. statement will tell the District Attorney who committed the crime
   D. the statement can be used as evidence

3. District Attorneys find that statements of a dying person are important, according to the above paragraph, because 3.____
   A. it may be that the victim will recover and then refuse to testify
   B. they are important elements in determining the mental attitude of the victim
   C. they present a point of view
   D. it may be impossible to punish the criminal without such a statement

4. A well-known gangster is found dying from a bullet wound. The patrolman first on the scene, in the presence of witnesses, tells the man that he is going to die and asks, *Who shot you?* The gangster says, *Jones shot me, but he hasn't killed me. I'll live to get him.* He then falls back dead. 4.____
   According to the above paragraph, this statement is
   A. *admissible* in evidence; the man was obviously speaking the truth
   B. *not admissible* in evidence; the man obviously did not believe that he was dying

C. *admissible* in evidence; there were witnesses to the statement
D. *not admissible* in evidence; the victim did not sign any statement and the evidence is merely hearsay

Questions 5-7.

DIRECTIONS: Questions 5 through 7 are to be answered SOLELY on the basis of the following paragraph.

The factors contributing to crime and delinquency are varied and complex. The home and its immediate environment have been found to be crucial in determining the behavior patterns of the individual, and criminality can frequently be traced to faulty family relationships and a bad neighborhood. But in the search for a clearer understanding of the underlying causes of delinquent and criminal behavior, the total environment must be taken into consideration.

5. According to the above paragraph, family relationships 5.____
A. tend to become faulty in bad neighborhoods
B. are important in determining the actions of honest people as well as criminals
C. are the only important element in the understanding of causes of delinquency
D. are determined by the total environment

6. According to the above paragraph, the causes of crime and delinquency are 6.____
A. not simple
B. not meaningless
C. meaningless
D. simple

7. According to the above paragraph, faulty family relationships FREQUENTLY are 7.____
A. responsible for varied and complex results
B. caused when one or both parents have a criminal behavior pattern
C. independent of the total environment
D. the cause of criminal acts

Questions 8-10.

DIRECTIONS: Questions 8 through 10 are to be answered SOLELY on the basis of the following paragraph.

A change in the specific problems which confront the police and in the methods for dealing with them has taken place in the last few decades. The automobile is a two-way symbol of this change in policing. It menaces every city with a complicated traffic problem and has speeded up the process of committing a crime and making a getaway, but at the same time has increased the effectiveness of police operations. However, the major concern of police departments continues to be the antisocial or criminal actions and behavior of human beings.

8. On the basis of the above paragraph, it can be stated that, for the most part, in the past few decades the specific problems of a police force 8.____
   A. have changed but the general problems have not
   B. as well as the general problems have changed
   C. have remained the same but the general problems have changed
   D. as well as the general problems have remained the same

9. According to the above paragraph, advances in science and industry have, in general, made the police 9.____
   A. operations less effective from the overall point of view
   B. operations more effective from the overall point of view
   C. abandon older methods of solving police problems
   D. concern themselves more with the antisocial acts of human beings

10. The automobile is a *two-way symbol*, according to the above paragraph, because its use 10.____
   A. has speeded up getting to and away from the scene of a crime
   B. both helps and hurts police operations
   C. introduces a new antisocial act—traffic violation—and does away with criminals like horse thieves
   D. both increases and decreases speed by introducing traffic problems

Questions 11-14.

DIRECTIONS: Questions 11 through 14 are to be answered SOLELY on the basis of the following passage on INSTRUCTIONS TO COIN AND TOKEN CASHIERS.

INSTRUCTIONS TO COIN AND TOKEN CASHIERS

Cashiers should reset the machine registers to an even starting number before commencing the day's work. Money bags received directly from collecting agents shall be counted and receipted for on the collecting agent's form. Each cashier shall be responsible for all coin or token bags accepted by him. He must examine all bags to be used for bank deposits for cuts and holes before placing them in use. Care must be exercised so that bags are not cut in opening them. Each bag must be opened separately and verified before another bag is opened. The machine register must be cleared before starting the count of another bag. The amount shown on the machine register must be compared with the amount on the bag tag. The empty bag must be kept on the table for re-examination should there be a difference between the amount on the bag tag and the amount on the machine register.

11. A cashier should BEGIN his day's assignment by 11.____
   A. counting and accepting all money bags
   B. resetting the counting machine register
   C. examining all bags for cuts and holes
   D. verifying the contents of all money bags

12. In verifying the amount of money in the bags received from the collecting agent, it is BEST to 12.____
    A. check the amount in one bag at a time
    B. base the total on the amount on the collecting agent's form
    C. repeat the total shown on the bag tag
    D. refer to the bank deposit receipt

13. A cashier is instructed to keep each empty coin bag on his table while verifying its contents CHIEFLY because, as long as the bag is on the table 13.____
    A. it cannot be misplaced
    B. the supervisor can see how quickly the cashier works
    C. cuts and holes are easily noticed
    D. a recheck is possible in case the machine count disagrees with the bag tag total

14. The INSTRUCTIONS indicate that it is NOT proper procedure for a cashier to 14.____
    A. assume that coin bags are free of cuts and holes
    B. compare the machine register total with the total shown on the bag tag
    C. sign a form when he receives coin bags
    D. reset the machine register before starting the day's counting

Questions 15-17.

DIRECTIONS: Questions 15 through 17 are to be answered SOLELY on the basis of the following passage.

The mass media are an integral part of the daily life of virtually every American. Among these media the youngest, television, is the most pervasive. Ninety-five percent of American homes have at least one T.V. set, and on the average that set is in use for about 40 hours each week. The central place of television in American life makes this medium the focal point of a growing national concern over the effects of media portrayals of violence on the values, attitudes, and behavior of an ever-increasing audience.

In our concern about violence and its causes, it is easy to make television a scapegoat. But we emphasize the fact that there is no simple answer to the problem of violence—no single explanation of its causes, and no single prescription for its control. It should be remembered that America also experienced high levels of crime and violence in periods before the advent of television.

The problem of balance, taste and artistic merit in entertaining programs on television are complex. We cannot countenance government censorship of television. Nor would we seek to impose arbitrary limitations on programming which might jeopardize television's ability to deal in dramatic presentations with controversial social issues. Nonetheless, we are deeply troubled by television's constant portrayal of violence, not in any genuine attempt to focus artistic expression on the human condition, but rather in pandering to a public preoccupation with violence that television itself has helped to generate,

15. According to the above passage, television uses violence MAINLY 15.____
    A. to highlight the reality of everyday existence
    B. to satisfy the audience's hunger for destructive action

C. to shape the values and attitudes of the public
D. when it films documentaries concerning human conflict

16. Which one of the following statements is BEST supported by the above passage? 16.____
A. Early American history reveals a crime pattern which is not related to television.
B. Programs should give presentations of social issues and never portray violent acts.
C. Television has proven that entertainment programs can easily make the balance between taste and artistic merit a simple matter.
D. Values and behavior should be regulated by governmental censorship.

17. Of the following, which word has the same meaning as *countenance*, as used in the above passage? 17.____
A. Approve B. Exhibit C. Oppose D. Reject

Questions 18-21.

DIRECTIONS: Questions 18 through 21 are to be answered SOLELY on the basis of the following passage.

Maintenance of leased or licensed areas on public parks or land has always been a problem. A good rule to follow in the administration and maintenance of such areas is to limit the responsibility of any lessee or licensee to the maintenance of the structures and grounds essential to the efficient operation of the concession, not including areas for the general use of the public, such as picnic areas, public comfort stations, etc.; except where such facilities are leased to another public agency or where special conditions make such inclusion practicable, and where a good standard of maintenance can be assured and enforced. If local conditions and requirements are such that public use areas are included, adequate safeguards to the public should be written into contracts and enforced in their administration, to insure that maintenance by the concessionaire shall be equal to the maintenance standards for other park property.

18. According to the above passage, when an area on a public park is leased to a concessionaire, it is usually BEST to 18.____
A. confine the responsibility of the concessionaire to operation of the facilities and leave the maintenance function to the park agency
B. exclude areas of general public use from the maintenance obligation of the concessionaire
C. make the concessionaire responsible for maintenance of the entire area including areas of general public use
D. provide additional comfort station facilities for the area

19. According to the above passage, a valid reason for giving a concessionaire responsibility for maintenance of a picnic area within his leased area is that 19.____
A. local conditions and requirements make it practicable
B. more than half of the picnic area falls within his leased area
C. the concessionaire has leased picnic facilities to another public agency
D. the picnic area falls entirely within his leased area

20. According to the above passage, a precaution that should be taken when a concessionaire is made responsible for maintenance of an area of general public use in a park is 20.____
   A. making sure that another public agency has not previously been made responsible for this area
   B. providing the concessionaire with up-to-date equipment, if practicable
   C. requiring that the concessionaire take out adequate insurance for the protection of the public
   D. writing safeguards to the public into the contract

KEY (CORRECT ANSWERS)

1.	B	11.	B
2.	D	12.	A
3.	D	13.	D
4.	B	14.	A
5.	B	15.	B
6.	A	16.	A
7.	D	17.	A
8.	A	18.	B
9.	B	19.	A
10.	B	20.	D

TEST 3

DIRECTIONS: Each question or incomplete statement is followed by several suggested answers or completions. Select the one that BEST answers the question or completes the statement. *PRINT THE LETTER OF THE CORRECT ANSWER IN THE SPACE AT THE RIGHT.*

Questions 1-5.

DIRECTIONS: Questions 1 through 5 are to be answered SOLELY on the basis of the following paragraph.

Physical inspections are an important tool for the examiner because he will have to decide the case in many instances on the basis of the inspection report. Most proceedings in a rent office are commenced by the filing of a written application or complaint by an interested party; that is, either the landlord or the tenant. Such an application or complaint must be filed in duplicate in order that the opposing party may be served with a copy of the application or complaint and thus be given an opportunity to answer and oppose it. Sometimes, a further opportunity is given the applicant to file a written rebuttal or reply to his adversary's answer. Often an examiner can make a determination or decision based on the written application, the answer, and the reply to the answer; and, of course, it would speed up operations if it were always possible to make decisions based on written documents only. Unfortunately, decisions can't always be made that way. There are numerous occasions where disputed issues of fact remain which cannot be resolved on the basis of the written statements of the parties. Typical examples are the following: The tenant claims that the refrigerator or stove or bathroom fixture is not functioning properly and the landlord denies this It is obvious that in such cases an inspection of the accommodations is almost the only means of resolving such disputed issues,

1. According to the above paragraph, 1.____
   A. physical inspections are made in all cases
   B. physical inspections are seldom made
   C. it is sometimes possible to determine the facts in a case without a physical inspection
   D. physical inspections are made when it is necessary to verify the examiner's determination

2. According to the above paragraph, in MOST cases, proceedings are started by a(n) 2.____
   A. inspector discovering a violation
   B. oral complaint by a tenant or landlord
   C. request from another agency, such as the Building Department
   D. written complaint by a tenant or landlord

3. According to the above paragraph, when a tenant files an application with the rent office, the landlord is 3.____
   A. not told about the proceeding until after the examiner makes his determination
   B. given the duplicate copy of the application

C. notified by means of an inspector visiting the premises
D. not told about the proceeding until after the inspector has visited the premises

4. As used in the above paragraph, the word *disputed* means MOST NEARLY 4.____
A. unsettled B. contested C. definite D. difficult

5. As used in the above paragraph, the word *resolved* means MOST NEARLY 5.____
A. settled B. fixed C. helped D. amended

Questions 6-10.

DIRECTIONS: Questions 6 through 10 are to be answered SOLELY on the basis of the following paragraph.

The examiner should order or request an inspection of the housing accommodations. His request for a physical inspection should be in writing, identify the accommodations and the landlord and the tenant, and specify <u>precisely</u> just what the inspector is to look for and report on. Unless this request is specific and lists <u>in detail</u> every item which the examiner wishes to be reported, the examiner will find that the inspection has not served its purpose and that even with the inspector's report, he is still in no position to decide the case due to loose ends which have not been completely tied up. The items that the examiner is interested in should be separately numbered on the inspection request and the same number referred to in the inspector's report. You can see what it would mean if an inspector came back with a report that did not cover everything. It may mean a tremendous waste of time and often require a re-inspection.

6. According to the above paragraph, the inspector makes an inspection on the order of 6.____
A. the landlord
B. the tenant
C. the examiner
D. both the landlord and the tenant

7. According to the above paragraph, the reason for numbering each item that an inspector reports on is so that 7.____
A. the report is neat
B. the report can be easily read and referred to
C. none of the examiner's requests for information is missed
D. the report will be specific

8. The one of the following items that is NOT necessarily included in the request for inspection is 8.____
A. location of dwelling
B. name of landlord
C. item to be checked
D. type of building

9. As used in the above paragraph, the word *precisely* means MOST NEARLY 9.____
A. exactly B. generally C. usually D. strongly

10. As used in the above paragraph, the words *in detail* mean MOST NEARLY 10.____
A. clearly B. item by item C. substantially D. completely

Questions 11-13.

DIRECTIONS: Questions 11 through 13 are to be answered SOLELY on the basis of the following passage.

The agreement under which a tenant rents property from a landlord is known as a lease. Generally speaking, leases are classified as either short-term or long-term in duration. They are further subdivided according to the method used to determine the amount of periodic rent payments. Of the following types of lease in use, the more commonly used ones are the following:

1. The straight or fixed lease is one in which rent may be paid in equal amounts throughout the duration of the lease. These are usually restricted to short-term leasing, or somewhat longer-term if clauses in the lease provide for periodic escalation of payments as the economy shifts.
2. Percentage leasing, used for short-term commercial leasing, provides the landlord with a stipulated percentage of a tenant's gross sales from goods and services sold on the premises, in addition to a fixed amount of rent.
3. The net lease, generally long-term (ten years or more), requires the tenant to pay all operating costs, including real estate taxes and insurance. In a net-net lease, the tenant further agrees to meet mortgage interest and principal payments.
4. An escalated lease, which is a long-term lease, requires rent to be of a stipulated base amount which periodically is subject to escalation in accordance with cost-of-living index scales, or in direct proportion to taxes, insurance, and operating costs.

11. Based on the information given in the passage, which type of lease is MOST likely to be advantageous to a landlord if there is a high rate of inflation? ______ lease. 11.____
    A. Fixed B. Percentage C. Net D. Escalated

12. On the basis of thee above passage, which types of lease would generally be MOST suitable for a well-established textile company which requires permanent facilities for its large operations? _____ lease and _____ lease. 12.____
    A. Percentage; escalated
    B. Escalated; net
    C. Straight; net
    D. Straight; percentage

13. According to the above passage, the ONLY type of lease which assures the same amount of rent throughout a specified interval is the _____ lease. 13.____
    A. straight B. percentage C. net-net D. escalated

Questions 14-15.

DIRECTIONS: Questions 14 and 15 are to be answered SOLELY on the basis of the following passage.

If you like people, if you seek contact with them rather than hide yourself in a corner, if you study your fellow men sympathetically, if you try consistently to contribute something to their success and happiness, if you are reasonably generous with your thought and your time, if you have a partial reserve with everyone but a seeming reserve with no one, you will get along with your superiors, your subordinates, and the human race.

By the scores of thousands, precepts and platitudes have been written for the guidance of personal conduct. The odd part of it is that, despite all of this labor, most of the frictions in modern society arise from the individual's feeling of inferiority, his false pride, his vanity, his unwillingness to yield space to any other man and his consequent urge to throw his own weight around. Goethe said that the quality which best enables a man to renew his own life, in his relation to others, is his capability of renouncing particular things at the right moment in order warmly to embrace something new in the next.

14. On the basis of the above passage, it may be INFERRED that 14.____
    A. a person should be unwilling to renounce privileges
    B. a person should realize that loss of a desirable job assignment may come at an opportune moment
    C. it is advisable for a person to maintain a considerable amount of reserve in his relationship with unfamiliar people
    D. people should be ready to contribute generously to a worthy charity

15. Of the following, the MOST valid implication made by the above passage is that 15.____
    A. a wealthy person who spends a considerable amount of money entertaining his friends is not really getting along with them
    B. if a person studies his fellow men carefully and impartially, he will tend to have good relationships with them
    C. individuals who maintain seemingly little reserve in their relationships with people have in some measure overcome their own feelings of inferiority
    D. most precepts that have been written for the guidance of personal conduct in relationships with other people are invalid

Questions 16-17.

DIRECTIONS: Questions 16 and 17 are to be answered SOLELY on the basis of the following passage.

When a design for a new bank note of the Federal Government has been prepared by the Bureau of Engraving and Printing and has been approved by the Secretary of the Treasury, the engravers begin the work of cutting the design in steel. No one engraver does all the work. Each man is a specialist. One works only on portraits, another on lettering, another on scroll work, and so on. Each engraver, with a steel tool known as a graver, and aided by a powerful magnifying glass, carefully carves his portion of the design into the steel. He knows that one false cut or a slip of his tool, or one miscalculation of width or depth of line, may destroy the merit of his work. A single mistake means that months or weeks of labor will have been in vain. The bureau is proud of the fact that no counterfeiter ever has duplicated the excellent work of its expert engravers.

16. According to the above passage, each engraver in the Bureau of Engraving and Printing 16.____
   A. must be approved by the Secretary of the Treasury before he can begin work on the design for a new bank note
   B. is responsible for engraving a complete design of a new bank note by himself
   C. designs new bank notes and submits them for approval to the Secretary of the Treasury
   D. performs sonly a specific part of the work of engraving a design for a new bank note

17. According to the above passage, 17.____
   A. an engraver's tools are not available to a counterfeiter
   B. mistakes made in engraving a design can be corrected immediately with little delay in the work of the Bureau
   C. the skilled work of the engravers has not been successfully reproduced by counterfeiter
   D. careful carving and cutting by the engraver is essential to prevent damage to equipment

Questions 18-21.

DIRECTIONS: Questions 18 through 21 are to be answered SOLELY on the basis of the following passage.

In the late fifties, the average American housewife spent $4.50 per day for a family of four on food and 5.15 hours in food preparation, if all of her food was *home prepared*; she spent $5.80 per day and 3.245 hours if all of her food was purchased *partially prepared*; and $6.70 per day and 1.64 hours if all of her food was purchased *ready-to-serve*.

Americans spent about 20 billion dollars for food products in 1941. They spent nearly 70 billion dollars in 1958. They spent 25 percent of their cash income on food in 1958. For the same kinds and quantities of food that consumers bought in 1941, they would have spent only 16% of their cash income in 1958. It is obvious that our food does cost more. Many factors contribute to this increase besides the additional cost that might be attributed to processing. Consumption of more expensive food items, higher marketing margins, and more food eaten in restaurants are other factors.

The Census of Manufacturers gives some indication of the total bill for processing. The value added by manufacturing of food and kindred products amounted to 3.5 billion of the 20 billion dollars spent for food in 1941. In the year 1958, the comparable figure had climbed to 14 billion dollars.

18. According to the above passage, the cash income of Americans in 1958 was MOST NEARLY _____ billion dollars. 18.____
   A. 11.2 B. 17.5 C. 70 D. 280

19. According to the above passage, if Americans bought the same kinds and quantities of food in 1958 as they did in 1941, they would have spent MOST NEARLY _____ billion dollars. 19.____
   A. 20 B. 45 C. 74 D. 84

20. According to the above passage, the percent increase in money spent for food in 1958 over 1941, as compared with the percentage increase in money spent for food processing in the same years, 20.____
   A. was greater
   B. was less
   C. was the same
   D. cannot be determined from the passage

21. In 1958, an American housewife who bought all of her food ready-to-serve saved time, as compared with the housewife who prepared all of her food at home 21.____
   A. 1.6 hours daily
   B. 1.9 hours daily
   C. 3.5 hours daily
   D. an amount of time which cannot be determined from the above passage

Questions 22-25.

DIRECTIONS: Questions 22 through 25 are to be answered SOLELY on the basis of the following passage.

Any member of the retirement system who is in city service, who files a proper application for service credit and agrees to deductions from his compensation at triple his normal rate of contribution, shall be credited with a period of city service previous to the beginning of his present membership in the retirement system. The period of service credited shall be equal to the period throughout which such triple deductions are made, but may not exceed the total of the city service the number rendered between his first day of eligibility for membership in the retirement system and the day he last became a member. After triple contributions for all of the first three years of service credit claimed, the remaining service credit may be purchased by a single payment of the sum of the remaining payments. If the total time purchasable exceeds ten years, triple contributions may be made for one-half of such time, and the remaining time purchased by a single payment of the sum of the remaining payments. Credit for service acquired in the above manner may be used only in determining the amount of any retirement benefit. Eligibility for such benefit will, in all cases, be based upon service rendered after the employee's membership last began, and will be exclusive of service credit purchased as described above.

22. According to the above passage, in order to obtain credit for city service previous to the beginning of an employee's present membership in the retirement system, the employee must 22.____
   A. apply for the service credit and consent to additional contributions to the retirement system
   B. apply for the service credit before he renews his membership in the retirement system
   C. have previous city service which does not exceed ten years
   D. make contributions to the retirement system for three years

23. According to the information in the above passage, credit for city service previous to the beginning of an employee's present membership in the retirement system is 23.____
    A. credited up to a maximum of ten years
    B. credited to any member of the retirement system
    C. used in determining the amount of the employee's benefits
    D. used in establishing the employee's eligibility to receive benefits

24. According to the information in the above passage, a member of the retirement system may purchase service credit for 24.____
    A. the period of time between his first day of eligibility for membership in the retirement system and the date he applies for the service credit
    B. one-half of the total of his previous city service if the total time exceeds ten years
    C. the period of time throughout which triple deductions are made
    D. the period of city service between his first day of eligibility for membership in the retirement system and the day he last became a member

25. Suppose that a member of the retirement system has filed an application for service credit for five years of previous city service. 25.____
    Based on the information in the above passage, the employee may purchase credit for this previous city service by making
    A. triple contributions for three years
    B. triple contributions for one-half of the time and a single payment of the sum of the remaining payments
    C. triple contributions for three years and a single payment of the sum of the remaining payments
    D. a single payment of the sum of the payments

KEY (CORRECT ANSWERS)

1. C
2. D
3. B
4. B
5. A

6. C
7. C
8. D
9. A
10. B

11. D
12. B
13. A
14. B
15. C

16. D
17. C
18. D
19. B
20. B

21. C
22. A
23. C
24. D
25. C

INTERPRETING STATISTICAL DATA GRAPHS, CHARTS, AND TABLES

EXAMINATION SECTION

TEST 1

DIRECTIONS: Each question or incomplete statement is followed by several suggested answers or completions. Select the one that BEST answers the question or completes the statement. *PRINT THE LETTER OF THE CORRECT ANSWER IN THE SPACE AT THE RIGHT.*

Questions 1-4.

DIRECTIONS: Questions 1 through 4 are to be answered on the basis of the following chart.

CENSUS DATA TOWNSHIPS IN ROCK COUNTY						
	2015			2020		
Townships	Pop.	% 65 years and over	% under 18 years	Pop.	% 65 years and over	% under 18 years
Smallville	43,095	27	?	45,045	30	?
Bedford	35,600	?	26	37,152	17	30
Hyatt	15,418	30	15	15,398	32	12
Burgess	75,400	21	?	82,504	9	?
Total	?	18	23	180,099	25	21

1. Approximately, what was the average population of the four townships in Rock County in 2015? 1.____
   A. 42,378
   B. 42,587
   C. 45,025
   D. Cannot be determined from information given

2. Which township experienced the LEAST population growth from 2015 to 2020? 2.____
   A. Smallville
   B. Bedford
   C. Burgess
   D. Cannot be determined from information given

3. In Rock County, in 2020, two out of every five individuals 18 years of age and over earn less than $32,000 a year. 3.____
   Approximately how many individuals are in this category?
   A. 37,821 B. 142,278 C. 56,911 D. 52,040

4. In Rock County, in 2020, 12966 people over 65 receive meals from the Senior Meals program. 4.____
If the participation rate is consistent throughout the county, approximately how many people over 65 are receiving meals in the Town of Hyatt?
   A. 1,232
   B. 1,419
   C. 2,879
   D. Cannot be determined from information given

Questions 5-8.

DIRECTIONS: Questions 5 through 8 are to be answered on the basis of the information shown in the following chart.

THE ECONOMY

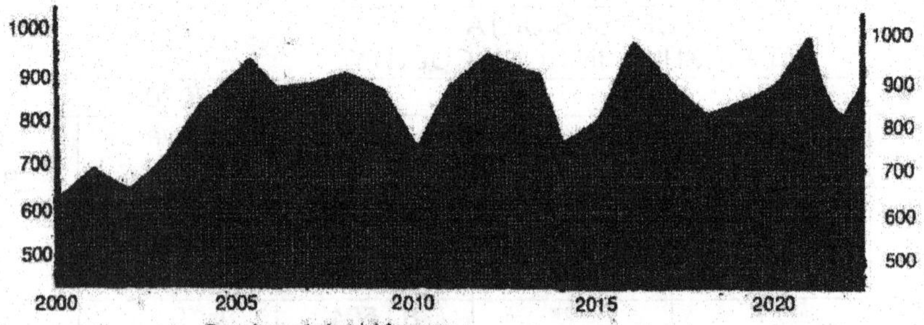

Dow Jones Industrial Average
Note: 2000-2020, annual averages; 2021-2022, quarterly averages

WHAT THE NUMBERS SAY: Both the prime rate and the mortgage interest rate are going down, and inflation is slowing somewhat. Unemployment keeps rising though, faster for Blacks than for Whites.

MONTHLY DATA	9/22	8/22	7/22	9/21	2007
Employment (seasonally adjusted)					
Number of unemployed (millions)	11.260	10.710	11.036	7.966	2.975
Overall unemployment rate	10.1%	8.6?	9.8%	7.5%	3.8%
Black unemployment rate	20.2%	18.8?	18.5%	15.1%	7.4%
Wages					
Average weekly earnings: current dollars	$270.05	$270.69	$269.98	$222.92	$101.84
Average weekly earnings: 2017 dollars	N/A	$168.50	$167.90	$144.94	$184.83
Prices					
All items Consumer Price Index	N/A	292.8	292.2	279.3	100.00
Increase from one year earlier	N/A	5.9%	6.5%	11.0%	2.9%
Food increase from on year earlier	N/A	3.6%	4.5%	6.5%	0.9%
Interest Rates					
Mortgage	14.99	15.68%	15.74%	15.37%	6.50%
Prime Interest Rate	13.50	14.39	16.26%	20.08%	5.61%

QUARTERLY DATA (billions of dollars at annual rates, seasonally adjusted)	2022 2nd	2022 1st	2021 2nd	2007
Gross National Product	3041.1	2995.5	2885.8	796.3
Balance of Trade (exports minus imports)	-20.47	-23.78	-24.9	+3.8
Wages, Salaries, and Benefits	1849.9	1830.8	1752.0	471.9
Corporate Profits	154.9	157.1	190.3	79.3
Gross National Product in 2012 dollars	1475.3	1470.7	1510.4	1007.7

NOTES: N/A means not available. Wages are the average for private sector nonfarm workers; no taxes have been subtracted. SOURCES: Employment, wages, and prices are from the Department of Labor Statistics. Mortgage interest rate is from the Federal Home Loan Bank Board. GNP and its components are from the Department of Commerce, Bureau of Economic Analysis.

5. The average weekly earnings, in 2017 dollars, for August of 2022, compared to the average weekly earnings, in 2017 dollars, for September of 2021, were 5.____
   A. $47.77 more
   B. $.60 more
   C. $47.77 less
   D. $23.56 more

6. The average weekly earnings, in current dollars, from September of 2021 increased 6.____
   A. 17.4%
   B. 21.4%
   C. 48%
   D. 16%

7. The Balance of Trade from 2007 to the 1st quarter of 2022 had declined approximately 7.____
   A. 13.8%
   B. 626%
   C. 726%
   D. 7.26%

8. From 2007 through September of 2022, the one category that has always shown an increase, of the following, is 8.____
   A. number of unemployed
   B. mortgage rates
   C. Black unemployment rate
   D. average weekly earnings: current dollars

Questions 9-12.

DIRECTIONS: Questions 9 through 12 are to be answered on the basis of the following chart.

	2009	2010	2011	2012	2013	2014	2015	2016
(Million Dollars)								
Food for development								
School lunch	137.3	106.9	123.3	102.5	79.169		66.3	?
Maternal and preschool feeding	31.4	37.4	51.3	48.8	45.0	54.3	90.5	?
Food for work	52.3	71.4	68.0	64.8	62.2	68.9	102.1	67.1
Total	221.0	215.7	242.6	2151.1	187.3	194.8	258.9	26.4
Emergency & Relief	55.7	47.3	60.2	182.7	?	88.1	57.9	45.3
Total, all programs	276.7	263.0	?	397.8	?	282.9	?	313.7
(Thousand Persons)								
Food for development								
School lunch	35,376	34,437	33,696	35,645	36,584	045	18,940	12,976
Maternal and preschool feeding	10,374	10,932	13,168	10,843	15,621	13,159	11,126	13,849
Food for work	12,884	14,193	10,992	15,260	10,970	8,799	8,481	8,175
Total	58,636	59,562	57,856	61,748	63,175	49,003	38,547	36,000
Emergency & Relief	14,012	18,083	17,467	28,143	23,715	6,406	12,759	4,025
Total, all programs	72,648	77,645	75,323	89,891	?	55,409	51,306	40,025

9. From 2010 to 2016, the value of exports designated for school lunches decreased 9.____
   A. 82 million dollars
   B. 56%
   C. 48.5%
   D. 94.4

10. The value of food exported for maternal and pre-school feeding amounted to the GREATEST per person in 10.____
   A. 2009
   B. 2010
   C. 2012
   D. 2016

11. If the total value of exports in 2017 decreased from the year before at the same rate as it changed from 2011 to 2012, the 2017 total equals MOST NEARLY _____ million. 11.____
   A. 100
   B. 413.7
   C. 210.2
   D. 417.2

12. The value of exported food for emergency and relief was $2.12 greater per person served in 2012 than in 2013. 12.____
What is the APPROXIMATE value of food exported for emergency and relief in 2013? _____ million.
   A. 103.6
   B. 204.2
   C. 10
   D. 91.3

Questions 13-16.

DIRECTIONS: Questions 13 through 16 are to be answered on the basis of the following chart.

THE 2012 BUDGET CUTS
(billions of dollars)

	2012 Original Budget	2012 Projected Outlays Obama Administration	
	Current Services (Outlays)	Amount	Change From Current Services
National Defense	$177.8	$187.5	$2
International Affairs	11.9	11.1	-0.8
General Science, Space & Technology	7.3	6.9	-0.4
Energy	11.8	6.4	-5.4
Natural Resources & Environment	13.8	12.6	-1.2
Agriculture	4.8	8.6	+3.8
Commerce & Housing Credit	5.1	3.3	-1.8
Transportation	21.9	21.2	-0.7
Community & Regional Development	?	8.4	0.8
Education, Training, Employment & Social Services	35.0	27.8	-7.2
Health	75.5	73.4	-2.1
Income Security	259.3	?	-8.4
Veterans Benefits & Services	24.4	24.2	-0.2
Administration of Justice	4.8	4.5	-0.3
General Government	5.2	5.1	-0.1
General Purpose Fiscal Assistance	6.5	6.4	-0.1
Interest	89.9	99.1	?
Contingencies for Other Requirements	-	1.0	-1.0
Allowances for Civilian Agency Pay Raises	3.2	0.4	-2.8
Undistributed Off-setting Receipts	-31.4	-31.6	-0.2
			gains +22.7
			cuts -33.5
			net $?
TOTAL	$?	$725.2	cut

13. By what percent did the 2012 Projected Outlays for National Defense increase from the 2012 original budget? 13.____
A. 9.7% B. 5.2% C. 5.5% D. 52%

14. What is the difference in outlays for Interest from the 2012 Original Budget to the Projected Outlays? 14.____
A. 1.2 billion dollars
B. $910,000
C. 9.2 million dollars
D. 9,200,000,000

15. For each dollar spent on Education, Training, Employment, and Social Services, according to the 2012 Original Budget, how much was to have been spent on National Defense? 15.____
A. $2.35 B. $.29 C. $.42 D. $5.08

16. The total change from Current Services is _____ billion dollars. 16.____
A. 736 B. -10.8 C. 10.2 D. 56.2

Questions 17-20.

DIRECTIONS: Questions17 through 20 are to be answered on the basis of the following chart.

TOWN RECREATION EXPENDITURES 2017-2019
(Hypothetical Data)

	2017	2018	2019
Personnel	$75,000	$82,000	$110,500
Special Events	6,110	6,730	6,860
May Day Festival	2,920	2,530	2,700
Baseball Marathon	3,190	4,200	4,160
Regular Programming	4,770	4,100	4,420
Music in the Park	1,200	1,200	1,350
Children's Theatre	1,580	1,300	1,320
Other	1,990	1,600	1,750
Park Maintenance	5,630	6,070	6,090
Playground Supplies	2,980	3,120	3,090
Landscaping	2,650	2,950	3,000
Total	$91,510	$98,900	$127,870
% Town Budget	3.8%	3.7%	3.6%

17. Of every ten dollars the town spent in 2018, approximately how much was spent on the Regular Programming category? 17.____
A. $0.37
B. $0.015
C. $0.255
D. Cannot be determined from information given

18. Town officials anticipate a 5% greater increase for 2020 personnel expenditures than the increase from 2018 to 2019. 18.____
Approximately what are the estimated 2020 personnel expenditures?
A. $154,479 B. $43,979 C. $143,979 D. $144,534

19. Approximately what percent of the entire town budget was spent on recreational Special Events in 2019? 19.____
    A. 3.6%
    B. 0.46%
    C. 0.2%
    D. Cannot be determined from information given

20. What area has seen the GREATEST rate of increase in expenditures between 2018 and 2019? 20.____
    A. Personnel
    B. Special Events
    C. Programming
    D. Park Maintenance

Questions 21-24.

DIRECTIONS: Questions 21 through 24 are to be answered on the basis of the following chart.

COMPARISON OF HOURLY WAGE RATES FOR FARMWORKERS AND PRODUCTION WORKERS IN MANUFACTURING, 2018-2020

	Production Workers in Mfg.			All Hired Farmworkers		Farmworker Wages as a Percentage of Mfg. Wages (In New York
	All Mfg.	Durable Goods	Non-durable Goods			
	NEW YORK			New York	U.S.	
2018						
January	$5.93	$6.46	$5.41	$2.85	$3.18	48%
April	5.99	6.52	5.46	2.71	3.09	45%
July	6.09	6.61	5.54	2.72	2.93	45%
October	6.14	6.77	5.49	2.90	3.18	47%
2019						
January	6.41	6.98	5.78	2.90	3.38	?
April	6.45	7.03	5.82	2.98	3.40	46%
July	6.58	7.17	5.95	2.80	3.23	43%
October	6.71	7.37	6.02	2.85	3.57	42%
2020						
January	6.91	7.50	6.26	3.10	3.69	45%
April	7.02	7.63	6.34	2.95	3.61	42%
July	7.11	7.76	6.42	2.86	3.52	
October	-	-	-	3.54	3.85	-

Farmworkers' piece rates are included in the above-listed figures.

21. For the four months given in 1980, hired farmworkers in the United States earned an average of 21.____
    A. $4.63
    B. $3.57
    C. $3.50
    D. $3.67

22. In New York, in July of 2020, the hourly wage paid farmworkers was what percent of the wage paid production workers in non-durable goods manufacturing? 22.____
    A. 41.3%
    B. 44.5%
    C. 54.8%
    D. 40.2%

23. The average wage for the four months given in 2018 of farmworkers hired in New York, as compared to all those hired in the United States, was 23.____
A. $.30 greater B. approximately 90% less
C. approximately 10% greater D. approximately 10% less

24. The hourly wages of hired farmworkers in New York in January of 2020, compared to the hourly wages of hired farmworkers in New York in October of 2019 increased 24.____
A. 45% B. 42% C. $.25 D. 15%

Questions 25-28.

DIRECTIONS: Questions 25 through 28 are too be answered on the basis of the following charts.

MULTIPLE JOBHOLDERS BY SEX, MARITAL STATUS, MAY 2018
COUNTY X

	Both Sexes			Men			Women		
	Total	Multiple Jobholders		Total	Multiple Jobholders		Total	Multiple Jobholders	
Characteristics	Employed	Number	Percent	Employed	Number	Percent	Employed	Number	Percent
Marital Status									
Single	23,123	1,015	?	13,031	6.16	4.7	10,092	398	3.9
Married, spouse present	61,121	3,142	5.1	38,080	2.356	6.2	23,041	786	3.4
Other marital status	12,565	603	4.8	4,671	237	5.1	7,894	364	?

MULTIPLE JOBHOLDERS BY TYPE OF INDUSTRY AND CLASS OF WORKER, MAY 2018
COUNTY X

	Multiple Jobholders			Second Job in Agriculture			Second Job in Nonagriculture		
Primary Job	Total Employed	Number	Percent of Employed	Total	Wage & Salary	Self-employed	Total	Wage & Salary	Self-employed
Total	96,809	4,758	4.9	722	173	549	4,036	3,024	1,012
Agriculture	3,458	180	5.2	?	42	25	113	107	6
Wage & Salary	1,455	67	4.6	44	19	25	23	17	6
Self-employed	1,677	94	5.6	23	23	(1)	71	71	(1)
Unpaid Family	326	20	6.1	0	0	(2)	20	20	(2)
Non-agriculture	93,351	4,578	4.9	?	131	524	3,923	2,917	1,006
Wage & Salary	86,024	4,328	5.0	649	124	524	3,680	2,674	1,006
Self-Employed	6,847	236	3.4	6	6	(1)	229	229	(1)
Unpaid Family	479	?	?	0	0	(2)	?	14	(2)

(1) Self-employed persons with secondary businesses or farms, but no wage or salary jobs, were not counted as multiple jobholders.
(2) Persons whose primary jobs were as unpaid family workers were counted as multiple jobholders only if they also held wage or salary jobs.

25. The ratio of married women with more than one job to all married multiple jobholders is 25.____
A. 1:3 B. 1:4 C. 3:1 D. 1:75

26. If 50% of those holding a second job in agriculture are men, how many men hold a second job in non-agriculture? 26.____
A. 2,848 B. 3,209 C. 2,488 D. 2,777

27. The percentage of agricultural workers who are self-employed compared to the percentage of non-agricultural workers who are self-employed is APPROXIMATELY 27.____
    A. two times greater
    B. seven times greater
    C. one-third less
    D. four times greater

28. 3.8% of the women and 5.8% of the men in the total labor force were multiple jobholders in May of 2018. 28.____
    If, in 2019, the total labor force increased by 10,955, with 40% of the new workers being women, but the percentage of male and female multiple jobholders remaining the same, how many more men than women were multiple jobholders in 2019?
    A. 3,617 B. 6,572 C. 1,891 D. 2,191

Questions 29-32.

DIRECTIONS: Questions 29 through 32 are to be answered on the basis of the following chart.

WORKERS AND DEPENDENTS, 1950-2050 AND BEYOND
CENSUS BUREAU TRENDS AND PROJECTIONS

Percentage of Total Population					Number of Dependents (Non-workers) Per Worker
	That is:				
Year	0-17	65+	18-64	Working	
1950	9	8.1	60.9	39.8	1.51
1960	35.7	9.2	55.1	37.8	1.65
1970	34.0	9	56.2	39.9	1.51
1979	?	11.2	60.4	44.9	1.23
2000	26.1	12.7	?	45.5	?
2025	24.0	18.2	57.8	43.0	?
2050	23.8	18.5	57.7	?	1.33

29. In the year 2050, dependents per worker is expected to have decreased from the number of dependents per worker in 1960 by 29.____
    A. .32 workers
    B. approximately 32%
    C. approximately 2%
    D. approximately 19%

30. If the percentage of the total population that is working in 2060 is 4.4% more than the percentage of the total population working in the year 2000, the percentage of the total population working in 2060 would be 30.____
    A. 49.9% B. 42% C. 41% D. 8%

31. If in 1982 the percentage of the total population that was 0-17 years of age had increased by 2% from the 1979 figure for this group, what was the percentage of the total population 0-17 years of age in 1982? 31.____
A. 45.6%
B. 12.3%
C. 30.4%
D. Cannot be determined from information given

32. In the year 2000, the number of dependents per worker is projected to be 32.____
A. approximately 1.18
B. approximately 1.20
C. approximately .83
D. Cannot be determined from information given

Questions 33-36.

DIRECTIONS: Questions 33 through 36 are to be answered on the basis of the following chart.

U.S. BALANCE OF TRADE, BY REGION, 2000, 2012, AND 2017
(Billions of Dollars)

				Change From	
	2000	2012	2017	2000-2012	2012-2017
World Total	?	-5.8	-26.7	-11.7	-20.9
Germany	+0.4	-1.4	?	?	+0.2
Other West Europe	+2.6	+1.4	+7.6	?	+6.2
Japan	+0.3	-4.1	-8.1	-4.4	-4.0
Other Developed	-1.1	-2.0	-1.8	-3.1	+0.2
Oil Companies	-0.6	-0.5	?	+0.1	-22.1
Taiwan	+0.5	-1.4	-4.0	?	-2.6
Other Third World	+1.1	+1.7		+0.6	-0.2
Communist Countries	+0.1	?	+1.6	+0.4	?

33. The U.S. Balance of Trade with Taiwan from 2000 to 2017 decreased 33.____
A. 1.9%
B. 2.6 billion dollars
C. 90%
D. 900%

34. In 2012, the value of the U.S. Balance of Trade with Communist countries, compared to the value of the U.S. Balance of Trade with the World total, was 34.____
A. 6.3 billion dollars greater
B. 10% greater
C. 5.3 billion dollars greater
D. cannot be determined from information given

35. If, in 2022, the U.S. Balance of Trade with Germany decreased by 40% from the 2017 figure, the U.S. Balance of Trade with Germany in 2022 35.____
A. decreased 48%
B. was -1.68 billion dollars
C. was -1.8 billion dollars
D. decreased by .78 billion dollars

36. If the 2000 World total of the U.S. Balance of Trade was 20% less than the World total of the U.S. Balance of Trade the year before it, then the U.S. Balance of Trade, World total, for 1999 was 36.____
   A. +7.080 billion dollars
   B. +6.431 billion dollars
   C. 7.375 billion dollars
   D. cannot be determined from information given

Questions 37-40.

DIRECTIONS: Questions 37 through 40 are to be answered on the basis of the following chart.

MARKET BASKET COMPARISON (JUNE 1, 2018)				
City	Food Cost	Tax (If Any)	Total	Approximate Difference from U.S. Average
Tampa	$32.58	0-0	$32.58	?
Des Moines	$33.80	0-0	33.80	?
San Diego	$34.02	0-0	$34.02	?
Phoenix	$33.19	?	$34.85	?
Atlanta	$34.60	4%-1.28	$35.98	-2.7%
Cleveland	$36.08	?	$36.08	-2.4%
Dallas	$36.41	0-0	$36.41	-1.5%
New York	$37.72	0-0	$37.72	+2.1%
Portland, Ore.	$38.10	0-0	$38.10	+3.1%
Chicago	$36.47	?	$38.29	+3.4%
Little Rock	$37.36	3%-1.12	$38.48	+4.1%
San Francisco	$38.82	0-0	$38.82	+5.0%
Philadelphia	$38.88	0-0	$38.88	+5.2%
Salt Lake City	$37.12	5%-1.86	$38.98	+5.5%
Washington, D.C.	$38.99	0-0	$38.99	+5.9%
Boston	$39.40	0-0	$39.40	+6.6%
Anchorage	$50.21	0-0	$50.21	+35.9%

37. The percentage of cities in the table that no tax was APPROXIMATELY 37.____
   A. 29%   B. 71%   C. 79%   D. 21%

38. If Portland, Oregon's Food Cost was approximately 3.1% more than the U.S. average, approximately what was the average Food Cost? 38.____
   A. $35.70   B. $36.92   C. $37.14   D. $36.95

39. In Phoenix, the amount of tax on the Food Cost category totaled 39.____
   A. 6%
   B. 5%
   C. 4%
   D. cannot be determined from information given

40. If the Food Cost of a market basket in San Francisco was $59.52 in 2019, then the Food Cost in San Francisco in 2019 compared to June 1 of 2018 increased 40.____
A. 20.7% B. $10.70 C. 53.3% D. 34.8%

KEY (CORRECT ANSWERS)

1.	A	11.	C	21.	D	31.	C
2.	B	12.	A	22.	B	32.	B
3.	C	13.	C	23.	D	33.	D
4.	B	14.	D	24.	C	34.	A
5.	D	15.	D	25.	B	35.	B
6.	B	16.	B	26.	A	36.	C
7.	C	17.	B	27.	B	37.	B
8.	C	18.	A	28.	C	38.	D
9.	C	19.	C	29.	D	39.	B
10.	D	20.	A	30.	A	40.	C

PREPARING WRITTEN MATERIAL

PARAGRAPH REARRANGEMENT COMMENTARY

The sentences that follow are in scrambled order. You are to rearrange them in proper order and indicate the letter choice containing the correct answer at the space at the right.

Each group of sentences in this section is actually a paragraph presented in scrambled order. Each sentence in the group has a place in that paragraph; no sentence is to be left out. You are to read each group of sentences and decide upon the best order in which to put the sentences so as to form a well-organized paragraph.

The questions in this section measure the ability to solve a problem when all the facts relevant to its solution are not given.

More specifically, certain positions of responsibility and authority require the employee to discover connection between events sometimes, apparently, unrelated. In order to do this, the employee will find it necessary to correctly infer that unspecified events have probably occurred or are likely to occur. This ability becomes especially important when action must be taken on incomplete information.

Accordingly, these questions require competitors to choose among several suggested alternatives, each of which presents a different sequential arrangement of the events. Competitors must choose the MOST logical of the suggested sequences.

In order to do so, they may be required to draw on general knowledge to infer missing concepts or events that are essential to sequencing the given events. Competitors should be careful to infer only what is essential to the sequence. The plausibility of the wrong alternatives will always require the inclusion of unlikely events or of additional chains of events which are NOT essential to sequencing the given events.

It's very important to remember that you are looking for the best of the four possible choices, and that the best choice of all may not even be one of the answers you're given to choose from.

There is no one right way to solve these problems. Many people have found it helpful to first write out the order of the sentences, as they would have arranged them, on their scrap paper before looking at the possible answers. If their optimum answer is there, this can save them some time. If it isn't, this method can still give insight into solving the problem. Others find it most helpful to just go through each of the possible choices, contrasting each as they go along. You should use whatever method feels comfortable and works for you.

While most of these types of questions are not that difficult, we've added a higher percentage of the difficult type, just to give you more practice. Usually there are only one or two questions on this section that contain such subtle distinctions that you're unable to answer confidently. And you then may find yourself stuck deciding between two possible choices, neither of which you're sure about.

EXAMINATION SECTION

TEST 1

DIRECTIONS: The sentences listed below are part of a meaningful paragraph, but they are not given in their proper order. You are to decide what would be the BEST order to put sentences to form a well-organized paragraph. Each sentence has a place in the paragraph; there are no extra sentences. *PRINT THE LETTER OF THE CORRECT ANSWER IN THE SPACE AT THE RIGHT.*

1. I. He came on a winter's eve. 1.____
   II. Akira came directly, breaking all tradition.
   III. He pounded on the door while a cold rain beat on the shuttered veranda, so at first Chie thought him only the wind.
   IV. Was that it?
   V. Had he followed form—had he asked his mother to speak to his father to approach a go-between—would Chie have been more receptive?

   The CORRECT answer is:
   A. II, IV, V, I, III B. I, III, II, IV, V C. V, IV, II, III, I D. III, V, I, II, IV

2. I. We have an understanding. 2.____
   II. Either method comes down to the same thing: a matter of parental approval.
   III. If you give your consent, I become Naomi's husband.
   IV. Please don't judge my candidacy by the unseemliness of this proposal.
   V. I ask directly because the use of a go-between takes much time.

   The CORRECT answer is:
   A. III, IV, II, V, I B. I, V, II, III, IV C. I, IV, V, II, III D. V, III, I, IV, II

3. I. Many relish the opportunity to buy presents because gift-giving offers a powerful means to build stronger bonds with one's closest peers. 3.____
   II. Aside from purchasing holiday gifts, most people regularly buy presents for other occasions throughout the year, including weddings, birthdays, anniversaries, graduations, and baby showers.
   III. Last year, Americans spent over $30 billion at retail stores in the month of December alone.
   IV. This frequent experience of gift-giving can engender ambivalent feelings in gift-givers.
   V. Every day, millions of shoppers hit the stores in full force—both online and on foot—searching frantically for the perfect gift.

   The CORRECT answer is:
   A. II, III, V, I, IV B. IV, V, I, III, II C. III, II, V, I, IV D. V, III, II, IV, I

4. I. Why do gift-givers assume that gift price is closely linked to gift-recipients' feelings of appreciation? 4.____
II. Perhaps givers believe that bigger (i.e., more expensive) gifts convey stronger signals of thoughtfulness and consideration.
III. In this sense, gift-givers may be motivated to spend more money on a gift in order to send a "stronger signal" to their intended recipient.
IV. According to Camerer (1988) and others, gift-giving represents a symbolic ritual, whereby gift-givers attempt to signal their positive attitudes toward the intended recipient and their willingness to invest resources in a future relationship.
V. As for gift-recipients, they may not construe smaller and larger gifts as representing smaller and larger signals of thoughtfulness and consideration.
The CORRECT answer is:
A. V, III, II, IV, I B. I, II, IV, III, V C. IV, I, III, V, II D. II, V, I, IV, III

5. I. But when the spider is not hungry, the stimulation of its hairs merely causes it to shake the touched limb. 5.____
II. Touching this body hair produces one of two distinct reactions.
III. The entire body of a tarantula, especially its legs, is thickly clothed with hair.
IV. Some of it is short and wooly, some long and stiff.
V. When the spider is hungry, it responds with an immediate and swift attack.
The CORRECT answer is:
A. IV, II, I, III, V B. V, I, III, IV, II C. III, IV, II, V, I D. I, II, IV, III, V

6. I. That tough question may be just one question away from an easy one. 6.____
II. They tend to be arranged sequentially: questions on the first paragraph come before questions on the second paragraph.
III. In summation, it is important not to forget that there is no penalty for guessing.
IV. Try *all* questions on the passage.
V. Remember, the critical reading questions after each passage are not arranged in order of difficulty.
The CORRECT answer is:
A. I, III, IV, II, V B. II, I, V, III, IV C. III, IV, I, V, II D. V, II, IV, I, III

7. I. This time of year clients come to me with one goal in mind: losing weight. 7.____
II. I usually tell them that their goal should be focused on fat loss instead of weight loss.
III. Converting and burning fat while maintaining or building muscle is an art, which also happens to be my job.
IV. What I love about this line of work is that *everyone* benefits from healthy eating and supplemental nutrition.
V. This is because most of us have more stored fat than we prefer, but we do not want to lose muscle in addition to the fat.
The CORRECT answer is:
A. V, III, I, II, IV B. I, IV, V, III, IV C. II, I, III, IV, V D. II, V, IV, I, II

8. I. In Tierra del Fuego, "invasive" describes the beaver perfectly. 8.____
   II. What started as a small influx of 50 beavers has since grown to a number over 200,000.
   III. Unlike in North America where the beaver has several natural predators that help to maintain manageable population numbers, Tierra del Fuego has no such luxury.
   IV. An invasive species is a non-indigenous animal, fungus, or plant species introduced to an area that has the potential to inflict harm upon the native ecosystem.
   V. It was first introduced in 1946 by the Argentine government in an effort to catalyze a fur trading industry in the region.

   The CORRECT answer is:
   A. IV, I, V, II, III B. I, IV, II, III, V C. II, V, III, I, IV D. V, II, IV, III, I

9. I. The words ensure that we are all part of something much larger than the here and now. 9.____
   II. Literature might be thought of as the creative measure of history.
   III. It seems impossible to disconnect most literary works from their historical context.
   IV. Great writers, poets, and playwrights mold their sense of life and the events of their time into works of art.
   V. However, the themes that make their work universal and enduring perhaps do transcend time.

   The CORRECT answer is:
   A. I, III, II, V, IV B. IV, I, V, II, III C. II, IV, III, V, I D. III, V, I, IV, II

10. I. If you don't already have an exercise routine, try to build up to a good 20- to 45-minute aerobic workout. 10.____
    II. When your brain is well oxygenated, it works more efficiently, so you do your work better and faster.
    III. Your routine will help you enormously when you sit down to work on homework or even on the day of a test.
    IV. Twenty minutes of cardiovascular exercise is a great warm-up before you start your homework.
    V. Exercise does not just help your muscles; it also helps your brain.

    The CORRECT answer is:
    A. I, IV, II, IV, III B. IV, V, II, I, III C. V, III, IV, II, I D. III, IV, I, V, II

11. I. Experts often suggest that crime resembles an epidemic, but what kind? 11.____
    II. If it travels along major transportation routes, the cause is microbial.
    III. Economics professor Karl Smith has a good rule of thumb for categorizing epidemics: if it is along the lines of communication, he says the cause is information.
    IV. However, if it spreads everywhere all at once, the cause is a molecule.
    V. If it spreads out like a fan, the cause is an insect.

    The CORRECT answer is:
    A. I, III, II, V, IV B. II, I, V, IV, III C. V, III, I, II, IV D. IV, V, I, III, II

12. I. A recent study had also suggested a link between childhood lead exposure and juvenile delinquency later on. 12.____
II. These ideas all caused Nevin to look into other sources of lead-based items as well, such as gasoline.
III. In 1994, Rick Nevin was a consultant working for the U.S Department of Housing and Urban Development on the costs and benefits of removing lead paint from old houses.
IV. Maybe reducing lead exposure could have an effect on violent crime too?
V. A growing body of research had linked lead exposure in small children with a whole raft of complications later in life, including lower IQ and behavioral problems.
The CORRECT answer is:
A. I, III, V, II, IV B. IV, I, II, V, III C. I, III, V, IV, II D. III, V, I, IV, II

13. I. Like Lord Byron a century earlier, he had learn to play himself, his own best hero, with superb conviction. 13.____
II. Or maybe he was Tarzan Hemingway, crouching in the African bush with elephant gun at the ready.
III. He was Hemingway of the rugged outdoor grin and the hairy chest posing beside the lion he had just shot.
IV. But even without the legend, the chest-beating, wisecracking pose that was later to seem so absurd, his impact upon us was tremendous.
V. By the time we were old enough to read Hemingway, he had become legendary.
The CORRECT answer is:
A. I, V, II, IV, III B. II, I, III, IV, V C. IV, II, V, III, I D. V, I, III, II, IV

14. I. Why do the electrons that inhabit atoms jump around so strangely, from one bizarrely shaped orbital to another? 14.____
II. And most importantly, why do protons, the bits that give atoms their heft and personality, stick together at all?
III. Why are some atoms, like sodium, so hyperactive while others, like helium, are so aloof?
IV. As any good contractor will tell you, a sound structure requires stable materials.
V. But atoms, the building blocks of everything we know and love—brownies and butterflies and beyond—do not appear to be models of stability.
The CORRECT answer is:
A. IV, V, III, I, II B. V, III, I, II, IV C. I, IV, II, V, III D. III, I, IV, II, V

15. I. Current atomic theory suggests that the strong nuclear force is most likely conveyed by massless particles called "gluons". 15.____
II. According to quantum chromodynamics (QCD), protons and neutrons are composed of smaller particles called quarks, which are held together by the gluons.
III. As a quantum theory, it conceives of space and time as tiny chunks that occasionally misbehave, rather than smooth predictable quantities.

IV. If you are hoping that QCD ties up atomic behavior with a tidy little bow, you will be disappointed.
V. This quark-binding force has "residue" that extends beyond protons and neutrons themselves to provide enough force to bind the protons and neutrons together.
The CORRECT answer is:
A. III, IV, II, V, I B. II, I, IV, III, V C. I, II, V, IV, III D. V, III, I, IV, II

16. I. I have seen him whip a woman, causing the blood to run half an hour at a time. 16.____
II. Mr. Severe, the overseer, used to stand by the door of the quarter, armed with a large hickory stick, ready to whip anyone who was not ready to start at the sound of the horn.
III. This was in the midst of her crying children, pleading for their mother's release.
IV. He seemed to take pleasure in manifesting his fiendish barbarity.
V. Mr. Severe was rightly named: he was a cruel man.
The CORRECT answer is:
A. I, IV, III, II, I B. II, V, I, III, IV C. II, V, III, I, IV D. IV, III, I, V, II

17. I. His death was recorded by the slaves as the result of a merciful providence. 17.____
II. His career was cut short.
III. He died very soon after I went to Colonel Lloyd's; and he died as he lived, uttering bitter curses and horrid oaths.
IV. Mr. Severe's place was filled by a Mr. Hopkins.
V. From the rising till the going down of the sun, he was cursing, raving, cutting, and slashing among the slaves in the field.
The CORRECT answer is:
A. V, II, III, I, IV B. IV, I, III, II, V C. III, I, IV, V, II D. I, II, V, III, IV

18. I. The primary reef-building organisms are invertebrate animals known as corals. 18.____
II. They are located in warm, shallow, tropical marine waters with enough light to stimulate the growth of reef organisms.
III. Coral reefs are highly diverse ecosystems, supporting greater numbers of fish species than any other marine ecosystem.
IV. They belong to the class Anthozoa and are subdivided into stony corals, which have six tentacles.
V. These corals are small colonial, marine invertebrates.
The CORRECT answer is:
A. I, IV, V, II, III B. V, I, III, IV, II C. III, II, I, V, IV D. IV, V, II, III, I

19. I. Jane Goodall, an English ethologist, is famous for her studies of the chimpanzees of the Gombe Stream Reserve in Tanzania. 19.____
II. As a result of her studies, Goodall concluded that chimpanzees are an advanced species closely related to humans.
III. Ultimately, Goodall's observations led her to write *The Chimpanzee Family Book*, which conveys a new, more humane view of wildlife.

IV. She is credited with the first recorded observation of chimps eating meat and using and making tools.
V. Her observations have forced scientists to redefine the characteristics once considered as solely human traits.
The CORRECT answer is:
A. V, II, IV, III, I B. I, IV, II, V, III C. I, II, V, IV, III D. III, V, II, I, IV

20. I. Since then, research has demonstrated that the deposition of atmospheric chemicals is causing widespread acidification of lakes, streams, and soil. 20.____
II. "Acid rain" is a popularly used phrase that refers to the deposition of acidifying substances from the atmosphere.
III. This phenomenon became a prominent issue around 1970.
IV. Of the many chemicals that are deposited from the atmosphere, the most important in terms of causing acidity in soil and surface waters are dilute solutions of sulfuric and nitric acids.
V. These chemicals are deposited as acidic rain or snow and include sulfur dioxide, oxides of nitrogen, and tiny particulates such as ammonium sulfate.
The CORRECT answer is:
A. III, IV, I, II, V B. IV, III, I, IV, V C. V, I, IV, III, II D. II, III, I, IV, V

21. I. Programmers wrote algorithmic software that precisely specified both the problem and how to solve it. 21.____
II. AI programmers, in contrast, have sought to program computers with flexible rules for seeking solutions to problems.
III. In the 1940 and 1950s, the first large, electronic, digital computers were designed to perform numerical calculations set up by a human programmer.
IV. The computers did so by completing a series of clearly defined steps, or algorithms.
V. An AI program may be designed to modify the rules it is given or to develop entirely new rules.
The CORRECT answer is:
A. I, III, II, V, IV B. IV, I, III, V, II C. III, IV, I, II, V D. III, I, II, IV, V

22. I. Wildfire is a periodic ecological disturbance, associated with the rapid combustion of much of the biomass of an ecosystem. 22.____
II. Wildfires themselves are both routine and ecologically necessary.
III. It is where they encounter human habitation, of course, that dangers quickly escalate,
IV. Once ignited by lightning or by humans, the biomass oxidizes as an uncontrolled blaze.
V. This unfettered burning continues until the fire either runs out of fuel or is quenched.
The CORRECT answer is:
A. V, IV, I, II, III B. I, II, V, III, IV C. III, II, I, IV, V D. IV, V, III, I, II

23. I. His arguments supported the positions advanced by the Democratic Party's southern wing and sharply challenged the constitutionality of the Republican Party's emerging political platform. 23.____
II. Beginning in the mid-1840s as a simple freedom suit, the case ended with the Court's intervention in the central political issues of the 1850s and the intensification of the sectional crisis that ultimately led to civil war.
III. During the Civil War, the decision quickly fell into disrepute, and its major rulings were overruled by ratification of the 13th and 14th Amendments.
IV. *Dred Scott v. Sandford* ranks as one of the worst decisions in the Supreme Court's history.
V. Chief Justice Roger Taney, speaking for a deeply divided Court, brought about this turn of events by ruling that no black American—whether free or enslaved—could be a U.S. citizen and that Congress possessed no legitimate authority to prohibit slavery's expansion into the federal territories.

The CORRECT answer is:
A. II, IV, I, III, V B. V, I, III, IV, II C. I, V, II, V, III D. IV, II, V, I, III

24. I. Considered the last battle between the U.S. Army and American Indians, the Wounded Knee Massacre took place on the morning of 29 December 1890 beside Wounded Knee Creek on South Dakota's Pine Ridge Reservation. 24.____
II. This was the culmination of the Ghost Dance religion that had started with a Paiute prophet from Nevada named Wovoka (1856-1932), who was also known as Jack Wilson.
III. During the previous year, U.S. government officials had reduced Sioux lands and cut back rations so severely that the Sioux people were starving.
IV. These conditions encouraged the desperate embrace of the Ghost Dance.
V. This pan-tribal ritual had historical antecedents that go much further back than its actual founder.

The CORRECT answer is:
A. I, II, III, IV, V B. V, IV, II, III, I C. IV, III, I, V, II D. III, I, V, II, IV

25. I. Their actions, which became known as the Boston Tea Party, set in motion events that led directly to the American Revolution. 25.____
II. Urged on by a crowd of cheering townspeople, the disguised Bostonians destroyed 342 chests of tea estimated to be worth between $10,000 an $18,000.
III. The Americans, who numbered around 70, shared a common aim: to destroy the ships' cargo of British East India Company tea.
IV. Many years later, George Hewes, a 31-year-old shoemaker and participant, recalled "We then were ordered by our commander to open the hatches and take out all the chests of tea and throw them overboard. And we immediately proceeded to execute his orders, first cutting and splitting the chests with our tomahawks, so as thoroughly to expose them to the effects of the water.

V. At nine o'clock on the night of December 16, 1773, a band of Bostonians disguised as Native Americans boarded the British merchant ship Dartmouth and two companion vessels anchored at Griffin's Wharf in Boston harbor.

The CORRECT answer is:

A. V, III, IV, II, I B. IV, II, III, I, V C. III, IV, V, II, I D. V, II, IV, III, I

KEY (CORRECT ANSWERS)

1. A
2. C
3. D
4. B
5. C
6. D
7. B
8. A
9. C
10. B
11. A
12. D
13. D
14. A
15. C
16. B
17. A
18. C
19. B
20. D
21. C
22. B
23. D
24. A
25. A

TEST 2

DIRECTIONS: The sentences listed below are part of a meaningful paragraph, but they are not given in their proper order. You are to decide what would be the BEST order to put sentences to form a well-organized paragraph. Each sentence has a place in the paragraph; there are no extra sentences. *PRINT THE LETTER OF THE CORRECT ANSWER IN THE SPACE AT THE RIGHT.*

1. I. Recently, some U.S. cities have added a new category: compost, organic matter such as food scraps and yard debris. 1.____
   II. For example, paper may go in one container, glass and aluminum in another, regular garbage in a third.
   III. Like paper or glass recycling, compositing demands a certain amount of effort from the public in order to be successful.
   IV. Over the past generation, people in many parts of the United States have become accustomed to dividing their household waste products into different categories for recycling.
   V. But the inconveniences of composting are far outweighed by its benefits.
   The CORRECT answer is:
   A. V, II, III, IV, I B. I, III, IV, V, II C. IV, II, I, III, V D. III, I, V, II, IV

2. I. It also enhances soil texture, encouraging healthy roots and minimizing the need for chemical fertilizers. 2.____
   II. Most people think of banana peels, eggshells, and dead leaves as "waste," but compost is actually a valuable resource with multiple practical uses.
   III. When utilized as a garden fertilizer, compost provides nutrients to soil and improves plant growth while deterring or killing pests and preventing some plant diseases.
   IV. In large quantities, compost can be converted into a natural gas that can be used as fuel for transportation or heating and cooling systems.
   V. Better than soil at holding moisture, compost minimizes water waste and storm runoff, increases savings on watering costs, and helps reduce erosion on embankments near bodies of water.
   The CORRECT answer is:
   A. II, III, I, V, IV B. I, IV, V, III, II C. V, II, IV, I,III D. III, V, II, IV, I

3. I. The street is a sea of red, the traditional Chinese color of luck and happiness. 3.____
   II. Buildings are draped with festive, red banners and garlands.
   III. Crowds gather then to celebrate Lunar New Year.
   IV. Lamp posts are strung with crimson paper lanterns, which bob in the crisp winter breeze.
   V. At the beginning of February, thousands of people line H Street, the heart of Chinatown in Washington, D.C.
   The CORRECT answer is:
   A. I, V, II, III, IV B. IV, II, V, I, III C. III, I, II, IV, V D. V, III, I, II, IV

4. I. Experts agree that the lion dance originated in the Han dynasty; however, there is little agreement about the dance's original purpose. 4.____
II. Another theory is that an emperor, upon waking from a dream about a lion, hired an artist to choreograph the dance.
III. Dancers must be synchronized with the music accompanying the dance, as well as with each other, in order to fully realize the celebration.
IV. Whatever the origins are, the current function of the dance is celebration.
V. Some evidence suggests that the earliest version of the dance was an attempt to ward off an evil spirt.
The CORRECT answer is:
A. V, II, IV, III, I B. I, V, II, IV, III C. II, I, III, V, IV D. IV, III, V, I, II

5. I. Half the population of New York, Toronto, and London do not own cars; instead they use public transport. 5.____
II. Every day, subway systems carry 155 million passengers, thirty-four times the number carried by all the world's airplanes.
III. Though there are 600 million cars on the planet, and counting, there are also seven billion people, which means most of us get around taking other modes of transportation.
IV. All of that is to say that even a century and a half after the invention of the internal combustion engine, private car ownership is still an anomaly.
V. In other words, traveling to work, school, or the market means being a straphanger: someone who relies on public transport.
The CORRECT answer is:
A. I, II, IV, V, III B. III, V, I, II, IV C. III, I, II, IV, V D. II, IV, V, III, I

6. I. "They jumped up like popcorn," he said, describing how they would flap their half-formed wings and take short hops into the air. 6.____
II. Dan settled on the Chukar Partridge as a model species, but he might not have made his discovery without the help of a local rancher that supplied him with the birds.
III. At field sites around the world, Dan Kiel saw a pattern in how young ground birds ran along behind their parents.
IV. So when a group of graduate students challenged him to come up with new data on the age-old ground-up-tree-down debate, he designed a project to see what clues might lie in how baby game birds learned to fly.
V. When the rancher stopped by to see how things were progressing, he yelled at Dan to give the birds something to climb on.
The CORRECT answer is:
A. IV, II, V, I, III B. III, II, I, V, IV C. III, I, IV, II, V D. I, II, IV, V, III

7. I. Honey bees are hosts to the pathogenic large ectoparasitic mite, *Varroa destructor*. 7.____
II. These mites feed on bee hemolymph (blood) and can kill bees directly or by increasing their susceptibility to secondary infections.
III. Little is known about the natural defenses that keep the mite infections under control.

IV. Pyrethrums are a group of flowering plants that produce potent insecticides with anti-mite activity.
V. In fact, the human mite infestation known as scabies is treated with a topical pyrethrum cream.
The CORRECT answer is:
A. I, II, III, IV, V B. V, IV, II, I, III C. III, IV, V, I, II D. II, IV, I, III, V

8. I. He hardly ever allowed me to pay for the books he placed in my hands, but when he wasn't looking I'd leave the coins I'd managed to collect on the counter. 8.____
II. My favorite place in the whole city was the Sempere & Sons bookshop on Calle Santa Ana.
III. It smelled of old paper and dust and it was my sanctuary, my refuge.
IV. The bookseller would let me sit on a chair in a corner and read any book I liked to my heart's content.
V. It was only small change—if I'd had to buy a book with that pittance, I would probably have been able to afford only a booklet of cigarette papers.
The CORRECT answer is:
A. I, III, V, II, IV B. II, IV, I, III, V C. V, I, III, IV, II D. II, III, IV, I, V

9. I. At school, I had learned to read and write long before the other children. 9.____
II. My father, however, did not see things the way I did; he did not like to see books in the house.
III. Where my school friends saw notches of ink on incomprehensible pages, I saw light, streets, and people.
IV. Back then my only friends were made of paper and ink.
V. Words and the mystery of their hidden science fascinated me, and I saw in them a key with which I could unlock a boundless world.
The CORRECT answer is:
A. IV, I, III, V, II B. I, V, III, IV, II C. II, I, V, III, IV D. V, IV, II, III, I

10. I. Gary King of Harvard University says that one main reason null results are not published is because there were many ways to produce them by messing up. 10.____
II. Oddly enough, there is little hard data on how often or why null results are squelched.
III. The various errors make the null reports almost impossible to predict, Mr. King believes.
IV. In recent years, the debate has spread to social and behavioral science, which help sway public and social policy.
V. The question of what to do with null results in research has long been hotly debated among those conducting medical trials.
The CORRECT answer is:
A. I, III, IV, V, II B. V, I, II, IV, III C. III, II, I, V, IV D. V, IV, II, I, III

11. I. In a recent study, Stanford political economist Neil Malholtra and two of his graduate students examined all studies funded by TESS (Time-sharing Experiments for Social Sciences). 11.____

II. Scientists of these experiments cited deeper problems within their studies but also believed many journalists wouldn't be interested in their findings.

III. TESS allows scientists to order up internet-based surveys of a representative sample of U.S. adults to test a particular hypothesis.

IV. One scientist went on record as saying, "The reality is that null effects do not tell a clear story."

V. Well, Malholtra's team tracked down working papers from most of the experiments that weren't published to find out what had happened to their results.

The CORRECT answer is:

A. IV, II, V, III, I B. I, III, V, II, IV C. III, V, I, IV, II D. I, III, IV, II, V

12. I. The work also suggests that these ultra-tiny salt wires may already exist in sea spray and large underground salt deposits. 12.____

II. Scientists expect for metals such as gold or lead to stretch out at temperatures well below their melting points, but they never expected this superplasticity in a rigid, crystalline material like salt.

III. Inflexible old salt becomes a softy in the nanoworld, stretching like taffy to more than twice its length, researchers report.

IV. The findings may lead to new approaches for making nanowires that could end up in solar cells or electronic circuits.

V. According to Nathan Moore of Sandia National Laboratories, these nanowires are special and much more common than we may think.

The CORRECT answer is:

A. IV, III, V, II, I B. I, V, III, IV, II C. III, IV, I, V, II D. V, II, III, I, IV

13. I. The Venus flytrap (Dionaea muscipula) needs to know when an ideal meal is crawling across its leaves. 13.____

II. The large black hairs on their lobes allow the Venus flytraps to literally feel their prey, and they act as triggers that spring the trap closed.

III. To be clear, if an insect touches just one hair, the trap will not spring shut; but a large enough bug will likely touch two hairs within twenty seconds which is the signal the Venus flytrap waits for.

IV. Closing its trap requires a huge expense of energy, and reopening can take several hours.

V. When the proper prey makes its way across the trap, the Dionaea launches into action.

The CORRECT answer is:

A. IV, I, V, II, III B. II, V, I, III, IV C. I, II, V, IV, III D. I, IV, II, V, III

14. I. These books usually contain collections of stories, many of which are much older than the books themselves. 14.____
    II. Where other early European authors wrote their literary works in Latin, the Irish began writing down their stories in their own language as early as 6th century B.C.E.
    III. Ireland has the oldest vernacular literature in Europe.
    IV. One of the most famous of these collections is the epic cycle, *The Táin Bó Culainge*, which translates to "The Cattle Raid of Cooley."
    V. While much of the earliest Irish writing has been lost or destroyed, several manuscripts survive from the late medieval period.

    The CORRECT answer is:
    A. V, IV, I, II, III B. III, II, V, I, IV C. III, I, IV, V, II D. IV, II, III, I, V

15. I. Obviously the plot is thin, but it works better as a thematic peace, exploring several great issues that plagued authors and people during that era. 15.____
    II. The story begins during a raid when Meb's forces are joined by Frederick and his men.
    III. In the end, many warriors on both sides perish, the prize is lost, and peace is somehow re-established between the opposing sides.
    IV. The middle of the story tells of how Chulu fends off Meb's army by herself while Concho's men struggle against witchcraft.
    V. The prize is defended by the current king, Concho, and the young warrior, Chulu.

    The CORRECT answer is:
    A. II, V, IV, III, I B. V, I, IV, III, II C. I, III, V, IV, II D. III, II, I, V, IV

16. I. However, sometimes the flowers that are treated with the pesticides are not as vibrant as those that did not receive the treatment. 16.____
    II. The first phase featured no pesticides and the second featured a pesticide that varied in doses.
    III. In the cultivation of roses, certain pesticides are often applied when the presence of aphids is detected.
    IV. Recently, researchers conducted two phases of an experiment to study the effects of certain pesticides on rose bushes.
    V. To start, aphids are small plant-eating insects known to feed on rose bushes.

    The CORRECT answer is:
    A. IV, III, II, I, V B. I, II, V, III, IV C. V, III, I, IV, II D. II, V, IV, I, III

17. I. My passion for it took hold many years ago when I happened to cross paths with a hiker in a national park. 17.____
    II. The wilderness has a way of cleansing the spirit.
    III. His excitement was infectious as he quoted various poetic verses pertaining to the wild; I was hooked.
    IV. For some, backpacking is the ultimate vacation.
    V. While it once felt tedious and tiring, backpacking is now an essential part of my summer recreation.

    The CORRECT answer is:
    A. IV, II, V, I, III B. II, III, I, IV, V C. I, IV, II, V, III D. V, I, III, II, IV

18. I. When I was preparing for my two-week vacation to southern Africa, I realized that the continent would be like nothing I have ever seen. 18.____
II. I wanted to explore the continent's urban streets as well as the savannah; it's always been my dream to have "off the grid" experiences as well as touristy ones.
III. The largest gap in understanding came from an unlikely source; it was the way I played with my host family's dog.
IV. Upon my arrival to Africa, the people I met welcomed me with open arms.
V. Aside from the pleasant welcome, it was obvious that our cultural differences were stark, which led to plenty of laughter and confusion.
The CORRECT answer is:
A. IV, I, II, III, V B. III, V, IV, II, I C. I, IV, II, III, V D. I, II, IV, V, III

19. I. There, I signed up for a full-contact, downhill ice-skating race that looked like a bobsled run. 19.____
II. It wasn't until I took a trip to Montreal that I realized how wrong I was.
III. As an avid skier and inline skater, I figured I had cornered the market on downhill speeds.
IV. After avoiding hip and body checks, both of which were perfectly legal, I was able to reach a top speed of forty-five miles per hour!
V. It was Carnaval season, the time when people from across the province flock to the city for two weeks of food, drink and winter sports.
The CORRECT answer is:
A. II, I, III, IV, V B. III, II, V, I, IV C. IV, V, I, III, II D. I, IV, II, V, III

20. I. It is a spell that sets upon one's soul and a sense of euphoria is felt by all who experience it. 20.____
II. Pictures and postcards of the Caribbean do not lie; the water there shines with every shade of aquamarine, from pastel to emerald.
III. As I imagine these sights, I recall one trip in particular that neatly captures the allure of the Caribbean.
IV. The ocean hypnotizes with its glassy vastness.
V. On that beautiful day, I was incredibly happy to sail with my family and friends.
The CORRECT answer is:
A. I, V, IV, III, II B. V, I, II, IV, III C. II, IV, I, III, V D. I, II, IV, III, V

21. I. It wasn't until the early 1700s that it began to resemble the masterpiece museum it is today. 21.____
II. The Louvre contains some of the most famous works of art in the history of the world including the *Mona Lisa* and the *Venus de Milo*.
III. Before it was a world famous museum, The Louvre was a fort built by King Philip sometime around 1200 A.D.
IV. The Louvre, in Paris, France, is one of the largest museums in the world.
V. It has almost 275,000 works of art, which are displayed in over 140 exhibition rooms.
The CORRECT answer is:
A. V, I, III, IV, II B. II, IV, I, V, III C. V, III, I, IV, II D. IV, V, II, III, I

22. I. It danced on the glossy hair and bright eyes of two girls, who sat together hemming ruffles for a white muslin dress. 22.____
II. The September sun was glinting cheerfully into a pretty bedroom furnished with blue.
III. These girls were Clover and Elsie Carr, and it was Clover's first evening dress for which they were hemming ruffles.
IV. The half-finished skirt of the dress lay on the bed, and as each crisp ruffle was completed, the girls added it to the snowy heap, which looked like a drift of transparent clouds.
V. It was nearly two years since a certain visit made by Johnnie to Inches Mills and more than three since Clover and Katy had returned home from the boarding school at Hillsover.

The CORRECT answer is:
A. III, V, IV, I, II B. II, I, IV, III, V C. V, II, I, IV, III D. II, IV, III, I, V

23. I. The "invisible hand" theory is harshly criticized by parties who argue that untampered self-interest is immoral and that charity is the superior vehicle for community improvement. 23.____
II. Standing as a testament to his benevolence, Smith bequeathed much of his wealth to charity.
III. Second, Smith was not arguing that all self-interest is positive for society; he simply did not agree that it was necessarily bad.
IV. First, he was not declaring that people should adopt a pattern of overt self-interest, but rather that people already act in such a way.
V. Some of these people, though, fail to recognize several important aspects of Adam Smith's the Scottish economist who championed this theory, concept.

The CORRECT answer is:
A. I, V, IV, III, II B. III, IV, II, I, V C. II, III, V, IV, I D. IV, III, I, V, II

24. I. Though they rarely are awarded for their many accomplishments, composers and performers continue to innovate and represent a substantial reason for classical music's persistent popularity. 24.____
II. It is often the subject of experimentation on the part of composers and performers.
III. Even more restrictive is the mainstream definition of "classical," which only includes the music of generations past that has seemingly been pushed aside by such contemporary forms of music as jazz, rock, and rap.
IV. In spite of its waning limelight, however, classical music occupies an enduring niche in Western culture.
V. Many people take classical music to be the realm of the symphony orchestra or smaller ensembles of orchestral instruments.

The CORRECT answer is:
A. IV, I, III, II, V B. II, IV, V, I, III C. V, III, IV, II, I D. I, V, III, IV, II

25. I. The Great Pyramid at Giza is arguably one of the most fascinating and contentious pieces of architecture in the world. 25.____
II. Instead of clarifying or expunging older theories about its age, the results of the study left the researchers mystified.
III. In the 1980s, researchers began focusing on studying the mortar from the pyramid, hoping it would reveal important clues about the pyramid's age and construction.
IV. This discovery was controversial because these dates claimed that the structure was built over 400 years earlier than most archaeologists originally believed it had been constructed.
V. Carbon dating revealed that the pyramid had been built between 3100 BCE and 2850 BCE with an average date of 2977 BCE.

The CORRECT answer is:
A. I, III, II, V, IV B. II, III, IV, V, I C. V, I, III, IV, II D. III, IV, V, I, II

KEY (CORRECT ANSWERS)

1. C
2. A
3. D
4. B
5. B

6. C
7. A
8. D
9. A
10. D

11. B
12. C
13. D
14. B
15. A

16. C
17. A
18. D
19. B
20. C

21. D
22. B
23. A
24. C
25. A

EXAMINATION SECTION

TEST 1

DIRECTIONS: The sentences listed below are part of a meaningful paragraph, but they are not given in their proper order. You are to decide what would be the BEST order to put sentences to form a well-organized paragraph. Each sentence has a place in the paragraph; there are no extra sentences. *PRINT THE LETTER OF THE CORRECT ANSWER IN THE SPACE AT THE RIGHT.*

Questions 1-3.

DIRECTIONS: Questions 1 through 3 are to be answered on the basis of the following passage.

Almost half of the increase in Chicago came from five neighborhoods, including West Garfield Park. He was 12 years old and had just been recruited into a gang by his older brothers and cousin. A decade later, he sits in Cook County jail, held without bail and awaiting trial on three cases, including felony drug charges and possession of a weapon. Violence in Chicago erupted last year, with the city recording 771 murders—a 58% jump from 2015. They point to a $95 million police-training center in West Garfield Park, public-transit improvements on Chicago's south side and efforts to get major corporations such as Whole Foods and Wal-Mart to invest. Chicago city officials say that they are making strategic investments in ailing neighborhoods. Amarley Coggins remembers the first time he dealt heroin, discreetly approaching a car coming off an interstate highway and into West Garfield park, the neighborhood where he grew up on Chicago's west side.

1. When organized correctly, the first sentence of the paragraph begins with — 1.____
   A. "Amarley Coggins remembers..."
   B. "He was 12 years old..."
   C. "They point to a..."
   D. "Violence in Chicago..."

2. After correctly organizing the paragraph, the author wishes to replace a word in the last sentence with its synonym *enterprises*. Which word does the author wish to replace? — 2.____
   A. murders
   B. neighborhoods
   C. corporations
   D. improvements

3. If put together correctly, the second to last sentence would end with the words — 3.____
   A. "...Chicago's west side."
   B. "...in ailing neighborhoods."
   C. "...older brother and cousins."
   D. "...and Wal-Mart to invest."

Questions 4-6.

DIRECTIONS: Questions 4 through 6 are to be answered on the basis of the following passage.

Critics argue that driverless vehicles pose too many risks, including cyberattacks, computer malfunctions, relying on algorithms to make ethical decisions, and fewer transportation jobs. Driverless vehicles, also called autonomous vehicles and self-driving vehicles, are vehicles that can operate without human intervention. And algorithms make decisions based on data obtained from sensors and connectivity. Driverless vehicles rely primarily on three technologies: sensors, connectivity, and algorithms. Sensors observe multiple directions simultaneously. Connectivity accesses information on traffic, weather, road hazards, and navigation. Supporters argue that driverless vehicles have many benefits, including fewer traffic accidents and fatalities, more efficient traffic flows, greater mobility for those who cannot drive, and less pollution. Once the realm of science fiction, driverless vehicles could revolutionize automotive travel over the next few decades.

4. When all of the sentences are organized in correct order, the first sentence starts with — 4.____
   A. "Connectivity accesses information..."
   B. "Critics argue that..."
   C. "Once the realm of..."
   D. "Driverless vehicles, also called..."

5. If the above paragraph appeared in correct order, which of the following transition words would be MOST appropriate in the beginning of the sentence that starts "Critics argue that..." — 5.____
   A. Additionally
   B. To begin,
   C. In conclusion,
   D. Conversely,

6. When the paragraph is properly arranged, it ends with the words — 6.____
   A. "...over the next few decades."
   B. "...fewer transportation jobs."
   C. "...and less pollution."
   D. "...without human intervention"

Questions 7-10.

DIRECTIONS: Questions 7 through 10 are to be answered on the basis of the following passage.

This method had some success, but also carried fatal risks. Various people across Europe independently developed vaccination as an alternative during the later years of the eighteenth century, but Edward Jenner (1749-1823) popularized the practice. Vaccination has been called a miracle of modern medicine, but it has a long and controversial history stretching back to the ancient world. In 1803 the Royal Jennerian Institute was founded in England, and vaccination programs initially drew enormous public support. In 429 BCE in Greece, the historian Thucydides (c.460-c.395 BCE) noted that survivors of smallpox did not become reinfected in subsequent epidemics. Variolation as a means of preventing severe smallpox infection became an accepted practice in China in the tenth century CE, and its popularity spread across Asia,

Europe, and to the Americas by the seventeenth century. Variolation required either inhalation of smallpox dust, or putting scabs or parts of the smallpox pustules under the skin. Widespread inoculation against smallpox was purported to have been part of Ayurvedic tradition as far back as at least 1000 BCE, when Indian doctors traveled to households before the rainy season each year.

7. When arranged properly, what does "This method" refer to in the sentence that begins "This method had some success..."? 7.____
   A. Vaccination B. Inoculation
   C. Variolation D. Hybridization

8. When organized correctly, the paragraph's third sentence should begin 8.____
   A. "In 429 BCE in Greece..." B. "Variolation required..."
   C. "In 1803 the..." D. "Vaccination has been called..."

9. If put in the correct order, this paragraph should end with the words 9.____
   A. "...under the skin." B. "...to the ancient world."
   C. "...enormous public support." D. "...by the seventeenth century."

10. In the second sentence, the author is thinking about using the word immunization instead of which of its synonyms? 10.____
   A. Variolation B. Vaccination C. Inhalation D. Inoculation

Questions 11-13.

DIRECTIONS: Questions 11 through 13 are to be answered on the basis of the following passage.

Summers are hot—often north of 100 degrees—and because it lies at the far end of a San Diego Gas & Electric transmission line, the town has suffered frequent power outages. Another way is that microgrids can ease the entry of intermittent renewable energy sources, like wind and solar, into the modern grid. Utilities are also interested in microgrids because of the money they can save by deferring the need to build new transmission lines. "If you're on the very end of a utility line, everything that happens, happens 10 times worse for you," says Mike Gravely, team leader for energy systems integration at the California Energy Commission. The town has a lot of senior citizens, who can be frail in the heat. Borrego Springs, California, is a quaint town of about 3,400 people set against the Anza-Borrego Desert about 90 miles east of San Diego. High winds, lightning strikes, forest fires and flash floods can bust up that line and kill the electricity. But today, Borrego Springs has a failsafe against power outages: a microgrid. Resiliency is one of the main reasons the market in microgrids is booming, with installed capacity in the United States projected to be more than double between 2017 and 2022, according to a new report on microgrids from GTM Research. "Without air conditioning," says Linda Haddock, head of the local Chamber of Commerce, "people will die."

11. When the sentences above are organized correctly, the paragraph should start with the sentence that begins 11.____
   A. "Borrego Springs, California..." B. "But today, Borrego Springs..."
   C. "Summers are hot..." D. "Utilities are also interested..."

12. If the author wanted to split this paragraph into two smaller paragraphs, the first sentence of the second paragraph would start with the words 12.____
    A. "High winds, lightning strikes, forest fires..."
    B. "But today, Borrego Springs..."
    C. "Resiliency is one of the main..."
    D. "If you're on the very end..."

13. Assuming the paragraph were organized correctly, the second to last sentence would end 13.____
    A. "...to build new transmission lines."
    B. "...be frail in the heat."
    C. "...into the modern grid."
    D. "...east of San Diego."

Questions 14-17.

DIRECTIONS: Questions 14 through 17 are to be answered on the basis of the following passage.

Exhaustive search is not typically a successful approach to problem solving because most interesting problems have search spaces that are simply too large to be dealt with in this manner, even by the fastest computers. Thus, in order to ignore a portion of a search space, some guiding knowledge or insight must exist so that the solution will not be overlooked. This partial understanding is reflected in the fact that a rigid algorithmic solution—a routine and predetermined number of computational steps—cannot be applied. A large part of the intelligence of chess players resides in the heuristics they employ. When search is used to explore the entire solution space, it is said to be exhaustive. Chess is a classic example where humans routinely employ sophisticated heuristics in a search space. Therefore, if one hopes to find a solution (or a reasonably good approximation of a solution) to such a problem, one must selectively explore the problem's search space. Rather, the concept of search is used to solve such problems. Heuristics is a major area of AI that concerns itself with how to limit effectively the exploration of a search space. Many problems that humans are confronted with are not fully understood. The difficulty here is that if part of the search space is not explored, one runs the risk that the solution one seeks will be missed. A chess player will typically search through a small number of possible moves before selecting a move to play. Not every possible move and countermove sequence is explored. Only reasonable sequences are examined.

14. When correctly organized, the paragraph above should begin with the words 14.____
    A. "Many problems that..."
    B. "Therefore, if one hopes to..."
    C. "Only reasonable sequences are..."
    D. "The difficulty here is..."

15. If the paragraph was organized correctly, the fourth sentence would begin with the words 15.____
    A. "Chess is a classic..."
    B. "Heuristics is a major..."
    C. "Exhaustive search is not..."
    D. "The difficulty here is..."

16. If the author wished to separate this paragraph into two equally sized paragraphs, the sentence that begins the second paragraph would END with the words 16.____
    A. "...heuristics they employ."
    B. "...in a search space."
    C. "...are not fully employed."
    D. "...will be missed."

17. When organized correctly, the paragraph would end with the words 17.____
    A. "...the heuristics they employ."
    B. "...will not be overlooked."
    C. "...said to be exhaustive."
    D. "...are not fully understood."

Questions 18-21.

DIRECTIONS: Questions 18 through 21 are to be answered on the basis of the following passage.

Asian-Americans soon found themselves the targets of ridicule and attacks. Prior to the bombing he had tried to enlist in the military but was turned down due to poor health. His case, Korematsu v. The United States, is still considered a blemish on the record of the Supreme Court and has received heightened scrutiny given the indefinite confinement of many prisoners after the terrorist attacks on September 11, 2001. On February 19, 1942, President Franklin D. Roosevelt issued Executive Order 9066, which granted the leaders of the armed forces permission to create Military Areas and authorizing the removal of any and all persons from those areas. Fred Korematsu was a 22-year-old welder when the Japanese bombed Pearl Harbor on December 7, 1941. A Nisei—which means an American citizen born to Japanese parents—he was one of four brothers and grew up working in his parents' plant nursery in Oakland, California. This statement effectively pronounced Japanese-Americans on the West Coast as traitors because even though Executive Order 9066 allowed the military to remove any person from designated areas, only those of Japanese descent were ordered to leave. Before Pearl Harbor, he was employed by a defense contractor in California. At the time of the attack, he was having a picnic with his Italian-American girlfriend. Asian-American Fred Korematsu (1919-2005) is most remembered for challenging the legality of Japanese internment during World War II. It was for this simple reason that he eventually became known as a civil rights leader. American reaction to an attack on United States' soil was both swift and harsh. Awarded the Presidential Medal of Honor, he is considered a leader of the civil rights movement in the United States. Roosevelt justified these actions in the opening paragraph of the order by declaring, "the successful prosecution of the war requires every possible protection against espionage, and against sabotage to national-defense material, national-defenses premises and national-defense utilities." Years later he told the San Francisco Chronicle, "I was just living my life, and that's what I wanted to do."

18. When put together correctly, the above paragraph would begin with the words 18.____
    A. "It was for this simple reason..."
    B. "A Nisei—which means..."
    C. "Awarded the Presidential Medal of Honor..."
    D. "Asian-American Fred Korematsu..."

19. If the author wished to separate this piece into two separate paragraphs, the sentence that would be the BEST way to start the second paragraph would begin with the words 19.____
    A. "Awarded the Presidential Medal of Honor…"
    B. "Fred Korematsu was a..."
    C. "Roosevelt justified these actions…"
    D. "Before Pearl Harbor, he was…"

20. In the sentence that begins "A Nisei—which means…", who does "he" refer to in the paragraph? 20.____
    A. Roosevelt
    B. A sibling of Korematsu
    C. Fred Korematsu
    D. Japanese-Americans on the West Coast

21. If organized correctly, the fourth sentence should begin with the words 21.____
    A. "At the time of the attack..."
    B. "His case, Korematsu v. The United States…"
    C. "Fred Korematsu was a…"
    D. "This statement effectively pronounced…"

22. When put together correctly, the last sentence of the paragraph should end with the words 22.____
    A. "…that's what I wanted to do."
    B. "…were ordered to leave."
    C. "…during World War II."
    D. "…was both swift and harsh."

Questions 23-25.

DIRECTIONS: Questions 23 through 25 are to be answered on the basis of the following passage.

Over the past two decades, her personal finances have been eroded by illness, divorce, the cost of raising two children, the housing bust, and the economic downturn. "There are more people attending college, more people taking out loans, and more people taking out a higher dollar amount of loans," says Matthew Ward, associate director of media relations at the New York Fed. Anderson, who is 57, told her complicated story at a recent Senate Aging Committee hearing (she's previously appeared on the CBS Evening News). Some 3 percent of U.S. households that are headed by a senior citizen now hold federal student debt, mostly debt they took on to finance their own educations, according to a new report from the Government Accountability Office (GAO), an independent agency. She hasn't been able to afford payments on her loans for nearly eight years. Rosemary Anderson has a master's degree, a good job at the University of California (Santa Cruz), and student loans that she could be paying off until she's 81. Student debt has risen across every age group over the past decade, according to a Federal Reserve Bank of New York analysis of credit report data… "As the baby boomers continue to move into retirement, the number of older Americans with defaulted loans will only continue to increase," the report warned. She first enrolled in college in her thirties.

23. When organized correctly, the first sentence should begin with the words 23.____
    A. "She first enrolled..."
    B. "Anderson, who is 57..."
    C. "Some 3 percent of..."
    D. "Rosemary Anderson has..."

24. If the author wished to split the paragraph into two paragraphs (not necessarily equal in length), the first sentence of the second paragraph would begin with the words 24.____
    A. "Some 3 percent of..."
    B. "There are more people..."
    C. "Over the past two decades..."
    D. "She first enrolled..."

25. When put in the correct order, the second to last sentence should end with the words 25.____
    A. "...an independent agency."
    B. "...of credit report data."
    C. "...at the New York Fed."
    D. "...in her thirties."

KEY (CORRECT ANSWERS)

1.	A	11.	A
2.	C	12.	B
3.	B	13.	C
4.	D	14.	A
5.	D	15.	C
6.	B	16.	D
7.	C	17.	A
8.	A	18.	D
9.	C	19.	B
10.	D	20.	C

21.	C
22.	B
23.	D
24.	A
25.	B

TEST 2

DIRECTIONS: The sentences listed below are part of a meaningful paragraph, but they are not given in their proper order. You are to decide what would be the BEST order to put sentences to form a well-organized paragraph. Each sentence has a place in the paragraph; there are no extra sentences. *PRINT THE LETTER OF THE CORRECT ANSWER IN THE SPACE AT THE RIGHT.*

Questions 1-3.

DIRECTIONS: Questions 1 through 3 are to be answered on the basis of the following passage.

According to the World Health Organization (WHO), exposure to ambient (outdoor) air pollution causes 3 million premature deaths around the world each year, largely due to heart and lung diseases. Air pollution also contributes to such environmental threats as smog, acid rain, depletion of the ozone layer, and global climate change. The U.S. Environmental Protection Agency (EPA) sets National Ambient Air Quality Standards (NAAQS) for those four pollutants as well as carbon monoxide (CO) and lead. The EPA also regulates 187 toxic air pollutants, such as asbestos, benzene, dioxin, and mercury. Finally, the EPA places limits on emissions of greenhouse gases like carbon dioxide (CO_2) and methane, which contribute to global climate change. The WHO has established Air Quality Guidelines (ACGs) to identify safe levels of exposure to the emission of four harmful air pollutants worldwide: particulate matter (PM), ozone (O_3), nitrogen dioxide (NO_2), and sulfur dioxide (SO_2). Since EPA criteria define the allowable concentrations of these six substances in ambient air throughout the United States, they are known as criteria air pollutants. Air pollution refers to the release into the air of chemicals and other substances, known as pollutants, that are potentially harmful to human health and the environment.

1. When organized correctly, the first sentence of this paragraph should begin 1.____
   A. "Air pollution refers..."
   B. "The EPA also regulates..,"
   C. "The WHO has established..."
   D. "According to the..."

2. When put in the correct order, the fourth sentence should end with the words 2.____
   A. "...to global climate change."
   B. "...as criteria air pollutants."
   C. "...nitrogen dioxide (NO_2), and sulfur dioxide (SO_2)."
   D. "...health and the environment."

3. If put in the most logical order, the paragraph would end with the words 3.____
   A. "...as criteria air pollutants."
   B. "...to global climate change."
   C. "...benzene, dioxin, and mercury."
   D. "...human health and the environment."

Questions 4-6.

DIRECTIONS: Questions 4 through 6 are to be answered on the basis of the following passage.

Although gentrification has been associated with some positive impacts, such as urban revitalization and lower crime rates, critics charge that it marginalizes racial and ethnic minorities and destroys the character of urban neighborhoods. British sociologist Ruth Glass is credited with coining the term "gentrification" in her 1964 book *London: Aspects of Change*, which described the transformation that occurred when members of the gentry (an elite or privileged social class) took over working-class districts of London. Gentrification is a type of neighborhood change, a broader term that encompasses various physical, demographic, social, and economic processes that affect distinct residential areas. The arrival of wealthier people leads to new economic development and an increase in property values and rent, which often makes housing unaffordable for longtime residents. Gentrification is a transformation process that typically occurs in urban neighborhoods when higher-income people move in and displace lower-income existing residents.

4. When organized in the correct order, the first sentence of the paragraph should begin with the words 4.____
   A. "Gentrification is a type of..."
   B. "British sociologist Ruth..."
   C. "The arrival of..."
   D. "Gentrification is a transformation..."

5. If put together in the correct order, the second to last sentence in the paragraph would end with the words 5.____
   A. "...lower-income existing residents."
   B. "...that affect distinct residential areas."
   C. "...character of urban neighborhoods."
   D. "...working-class districts of London."

6. If the author wished to change the beginning of the final sentence to "in the end." to better signal the finish of the paragraph, which of the following words would the phrase appear in front of? 6.____
   A. British
   B. Gentrification
   C. Although
   D. The

Questions 7-11.

DIRECTIONS: Questions 7 through 11 are to be answered on the basis of the following passage.

The primary signs of ADHD include a persistent pattern of inattention or hyperactivity lasting in duration for six months or longer with an onset before 12 years of age. Children with ADHD often experience peer rejection, neglect, or teasing and family interactions may contain high levels of discord and negative interactions (APA, 2013). Two primary types of the disorder include inattentive and hyperactive/impulsive, with a combined type when both inattention and hyperactivity occur together. Inattentive ADHD is evidenced by executive functioning deficits such as being off task, lacking sustained focus, and being disorganized. Hyperactive ADHD is evidenced by excessive talkativeness and fidgeting, with an inability to control impulses that may result in harm. Attention Deficit Hyperactivity Disorder (ADHD) is a commonly diagnosed childhood behavioral disorder affecting millions of children in the U.S. every year (National Institute of Mental Health [NIMH], 2012), with prevalence rates between 5% and 11% of the population. Other research has examined singular traits such as executive function deficits in the school setting, task performance in the school setting (Berk, 1986), driving and awareness of time. However, researching academic aspects of the school experience does not provide a comprehensive understanding of the systemic effects of ADHD in the school environment. Historically, much research on ADHD has focused on the academic impact of behavioral symptoms such as reading and mathematics. These behaviors are inappropriate for the child's age level and symptoms typically interfere with functioning in multiple environments.

7. If the author put the paragraph into a logical order, the first sentence would begin with the words 7.____
   A. "Inattentive ADHD is..."
   B. "Historically, much research..."
   C. "These behaviors are..."
   D. "Attention Deficit Hyperactivity Disorder..."

8. When put in the correct order, what does the author mean by "These behaviors" in the sentence that begins "These behaviors are..."? 8.____
   A. Inattention or hyperactivity
   B. Reading and Mathematics
   C. Peer rejection
   D. Sustained focus

9. If the author wished to split this paragraph into two paragraphs (not necessarily equal parts), the first sentence of the second paragraph would BEGIN with the words 9.____
   A. "Historically, much research..."
   B. "Other research has examined..."
   C. "Two primary types of..."
   D. "Inattentive ADHD is evidenced..."

10. When put in the correct order, the third sentence in the paragraph would END with the words 10.____
   A. "...an onset before 12 years of age."
   B. "...5% and 11% of the population."
   C. "...such as reading and mathematics."
   D. "...in multiple environments."

11. If the above paragraph was organized correctly, its ending words of the last sentence would be 11.____
   A. "...sustained focus, and being disorganized."
   B. "...an onset before 12 years of age."
   C. "...in the school environment."
   D. "...inattention and hyperactivity occur together."

Questions 12-15.

DIRECTIONS: Questions 12 through 15 are to be answered on the basis of the following passage.

Health care fraud imposes huge costs on society. In prosecutions of fraud, the DOJ employs the resources of its own criminal and civil divisions, as well as those of the U.S. Attorneys' Offices, HHS, and the FBI. The FBI estimates that health care fraud accounts for at least three and possibly up to ten percent of total health care expenditures, or somewhere between $82 billion and $272 billion each year. Providers are also careful to screen hires for excluded persons or entities lest they be subject to civil monetary penalties. Several government agencies are involved in fighting health care fraud. Individual states assist the HHS Office of the Inspector General ("OIG") and Centers for Medicare & Medicaid Services ("CMS") to initiate and pursue investigations of Medicare and Medicaid fraud. In addition, the OIG uses its permissive exclusion authority to exclude individuals and entities convicted of health care related crimes from federally funded health care services in order to induce providers to help track fraud through a voluntary disclosure program. $30 to $98 billion dollars of that (approximately 36%) is fraud against the public health programs Medicare and Medicaid. The Department of Justice ("DOJ") and the Department of Health and Human Services ("HHS") enforce federal health care fraud law and regulations.

12. When put together in a logical order, the second sentence of the paragraph would end with the words 12.____
   A. "...in fighting health care fraud."
   B. "...$272 billion each year."
   C. "...voluntary disclosure program."
   D. "...to civil monetary penalties."

13. In order to organize the paragraph correctly, the sentence that begins "In addition, the OIG..." should FOLLOW the sentence that begins with the words 13.____
   A. "$30 to $98 billion dollars of that..."
   B. "Health care fraud..."
   C. "Individual states assist..."
   D. "In prosecutions of fraud..."

14. The author wishes to split the paragraph into a smaller introductory paragraph followed by a slightly longer body paragraph. Which of the following sentences would be BEST to start the second paragraph? 14.____
   A. "$30 to $98 billion dollars of that (approximately 36%) is fraud against the public health care programs Medicare and Medicaid."
   B. "Several government agencies are involved in fighting health care fraud."
   C. "In prosecutions of fraud, the DOJ employs the resources of its own criminal and civil divisions, as well as those of the U.S. Attorneys' Offices, HHS, and the FBI."
   D. "Health care fraud imposes huge costs on society."

15. If put together correctly, the paragraph should end with the words 15.____
    A. "...Attorneys' Offices, HHS, and the FBI."
    B. "...huge costs on society."
    C. "...fighting health care fraud."
    D. "...of Medicare and Medicaid fraud."

Questions 16-19.

DIRECTIONS: Questions 16 through 19 are to be answered on the basis of the following passage.

President Abraham Lincoln advocated for granting amnesty to former Confederates to heal the country after the devastating war. Adams and his fellow Federalist Party members in Congress used the law to jail more than a dozen of his political rivals. In 1977, President Jimmy Carter lifted the restrictions on draft dodgers, granting them unconditional amnesty. The issue of amnesty again arose shortly after the U.S. Civil War (1861-1865). Some U.S. government officials, including Vice President Andrew Johnson, advocating placing severe punishments on the military and civilian leaders of the secessionist Confederate States of America. A century later, the controversial nature of the Vietnam War (1964-1975), combined with the compulsory draft for military service, compelled many young men of eligible age to violate the law to avoid the draft. When Thomas Jefferson, Adams' Vice President and opponent of the Alien and Sedition Acts, won the 1800 presidential election, he declared amnesty for those found to have violated the law. Other young men who were drafted deserted the army and refused to serve. In May 1865, when serving as president following Lincoln's assassination, Johnson issued the Proclamation of Amnesty and Reconstruction, which granted the rights of voting and holding office to most former Confederates. In 1974, President Gerald Ford granted amnesty to deserters and "draft dodgers" on the condition that they swear allegiance to the United States and engage in two years of community service. In 1798, President John Adams signed the Alien and Sedition Acts, a set of four laws that restricted criticism of the federal government.

16. When put in the correct order, the paragraph would begin with the following words. 16.____
    A. "Some U.S. government..."
    B. "In May 1865, when..."
    C. "A century later, the..."
    D. "In 1798, President..."

17. If put in logical order, what sentence number would the sentence that begins "President Abraham Lincoln..." be? 17.____
    A. One
    B. Six
    C. Five
    D. Two

18. The author wants to split this paragraph into three separate paragraphs. The THIRD paragraph should begin with the words 18.____
    A. "The issue of amnesty again..."
    B. "In 1798, President..."
    C. "In 1977, President Jimmy..."
    D. "A century later, the..."

19. When organized in sequential order, the last sentence of the paragraph would end with the words 19.____
    A. "...of his political rivals."
    B. "...after the devastating war."
    C. "...them unconditional amnesty."
    D. "...of the federal government."

Questions 20-22.

DIRECTIONS: Questions 20 through 22 are to be answered on the basis of the following passage.

Throughout history, militias have played an important role in national defense against foreign invaders or oppressors. In the original American colonies, state militias served to keep order and played an important role in the fight for independence from the British during the American Revolutionary War. Since that time, state-level militias have continued to exist in the United States alongside a national standing army, providing additional reserve defense and emergency assistance when needed. Some countries still rely almost entirely on public militias for civil defense. In Switzerland, for example, all able-bodied males must serve as part of the Swiss military or civilian service for several months starting when they turn 20 years old and remain reserve militia for years after. Similarly, in Israel, all non-Arab citizens over the age of 18 are required to serve in the Israel Defense Forces for at least two years; Israel is unique in that it requires military service from female citizens as well as males.

20. When put into the correct order, the paragraph should begin with the words 20.____
    A. "Throughout history, militias..."
    B. "Similarly, in Israel..."
    C. "Some countries still rely..."
    D. "Since that time, state-level..."

21. The fifth sentence of the paragraph should end with the words 21.____
    A. "...against foreign invaders or oppressors."
    B. "...militias for civil defense."
    C. "...reserve militia for years after."
    D. "...citizens as well as males."

22. The last sentence of the paragraph should end with the words 22.____
    A. "...militias for civil defense."
    B. "...citizens as well as males."
    C. "...against foreign invaders or oppressors."
    D. "...during the American Revolutionary War."

Questions 23-25.

DIRECTIONS: Questions 23 through 25 are to be answered on the basis of the following passage.

Medicines such as herbal and homeopathic remedies differ radically from those typically prescribed by mainstream physicians. These practices derive from different cultural traditions and scientific premises. As of 2012, the Memorial Sloan-Kettering Cancer Center offered hypnosis and tai chi, which is an ancient Chinese exercise, to help eases the pains associated with conventional cancer treatments. Some medical professionals staunchly dismiss a number of alternative techniques and theories as quackery. The concept of alternative medicine encompasses an extremely wide range of therapeutic modalities, from acupuncture to yoga. As of 2012, nearly 40 percent of Americans use some alternative medicines or therapies, according to the National Institutes of Health's National Center for Complementary and Alternative Medicine. Alternative approaches to health, fitness, disease prevention, and treatment are sometimes referred to as holistic health care or natural medicine. These names suggest some of the philosophical foundations shared by traditions such as homeopathy, naturopathy, traditional Chinese medicine and herbal medicine. A University of Pennsylvania study in 2010 found that more than 70 percent of U.S. cancer centers offered information on complementary therapies. Increasingly, health care providers are encouraging patients to combine alternative and conventional (or allopathic) treatments, a practice known as complementary or integrative medicine. In the contemporary United States, the phrase alternative medicine has come to mean virtually any healing or wellness practice not based within the conventional system of medical doctors, nurses, and hospitals. Some of these alternative treatments include acupuncture to alleviate pain and nausea and yoga to help reduce stress and manage pain. Yet taken as a whole, the alternative sector of the health field is enormously popular and rapidly growing. The Health Services Research Journal reported in 2011 that three out of four U.S. health care workers used complementary or alternative medicine practices themselves. Other studies have shown that more medical professionals are recommending that cancer patients seek alternative treatments to deal with the side effects of conventional treatments, such as chemotherapy, radiation, and surgery.

23. When put in the correct order, the first sentence should begin with the words 23.____
    A. "A University of Pennsylvania study…"
    B. "Other studies have shown that…"
    C. "Increasingly, health care providers…"
    D. "In the contemporary United States…"

24. If the author were to split the paragraph into two separate ones, the first sentence of the second paragraph should begin with the words 24.____
    A. "Alternative approaches to health…"
    B. "The concept of alternative medicine…"
    C. "As of 2012, nearly 40%..."
    D. "These names suggest some…"

25. When put into the correct logical sequence, the paragraph should end with the words 25.____
    A. "…Complementary and Alternative Medicine."
    B. "…system of medical doctors, nurses, and hospitals."
    C. "…associated with conventional cancer treatments."
    D. "…health care or natural medicine."

KEY (CORRECT ANSWERS)

1. A
2. C
3. B
4. D
5. B

6. C
7. D
8. A
9. A
10. D

11. C
12. B
13. C
14. B
15. A

16. D
17. B
18. D
19. C
20. A

21. C
22. B
23. D
24. A
25. C